Guess Again,
Sherlock

Deductive Reasoning —
An Elementary Guide

by

Stephen Pape

FOR PRIVATE DEDUCTIVES EVERYWHERE.

Contents

Let's begin with an old joke 1

Why bother with reasoning? 4

The basic plot.. 8

The three main characters...12

    Inductive reasoning – an outline.....................................13

    Abductive reasoning – an outline....................................16

    Deductive reasoning – an outline....................................18

Our new best friend..20

    Quantifiers 22

    Subject and predicate..23

    Major term, minor term, middle term...........................24

The sign of four 27

    Figure 1 syllogism..27

    Figure 2 syllogism..28

    Figure 3 syllogism..28

    Figure 4 syllogism..28

    Shorthand for syllogisms...29

Nothing but the truth 31

    Valid figure 1 syllogisms 31

    Valid figure 2 syllogisms 33

    Valid figure 3 syllogisms 34

    Valid figure 4 syllogisms 35

A handy crib sheet 38

Why nine out of ten syllogisms don't work........40

    Existential fallacy 41

    Four terms – fallacy..44

Undistributed middle– fallacy 45

'Distributed' has a particular meaning.........................46

Undistributed middle – part 2 49

Illicit major...50

Illicit minor 51

Exclusive premises 52

Affirmative conclusion – one negative premise........53

Negative conclusion – two affirmative premises.....53

A last look around before we go 54

Hypothetical arguments 55

Affirming the consequent 57

Denying the consequent...59

Denying the antecedent..61

Affirming the antecedent 62

Necessary conditions...64

Sufficient conditions 66

Conditions both necessary and sufficient...................67

The fallacy of necessity..68

Either ... or 71

Affirming or denying a disjunct.......................................71

Inclusive-or..72

Joined-up connections..74

Other formal fallacies 76

Bad reasons fallacy 76

Appeal to probability...76

Base rate fallacy 77

Proof by example..81

Conjunction fallacy 83

Masked man fallacy 84

When to apply deductive mode 90

Confirm the premises of any argument 90

Wrinkles in the cloth of reasoning 91

Informal fallacies 94

Whatever puffs up your lilo 95

Wear your learning lightly 96

LET'S BEGIN WITH AN OLD JOKE

One thing lovers of amateur sleuthing believe is that Sherlock Holmes was the embodiment of deductive reasoning. This may come as a shock to devotees – Sherlock knew nothing about deduction. It was an unopened email to the great detective. To explain, let's re-hash the old Sherlock and Watson gag:

> Sherlock Holmes and Dr Watson are on a camping holiday. In the middle of the night, Sherlock wakes and addresses his amanuensis: "Tell me, Watson, what do you observe and deduce?"
>
> "Well, Holmes, I see millions of beautiful stars, and from the constellations I observe, I deduce we are in the northern hemisphere, roughly fifty-two degrees north of the equator."
>
> "Very good, Watson," Holmes says, "anything else?"
>
> "Well, I see the sky is completely dark, so I deduce the hour is not yet four-seventeen in the morning when the first rays of dawn will approach our latitude and longitude at this time of year."
>
> "Very good," Holmes says, "anything else?"
>
> "Noting the humidity and cool, clear night, I predict there will be some dewfall in the morning but, without cloud, it will commence as a bright sunny day. Would you agree, Holmes?"
>
> "Yes, Watson, and precisely because you are able to deduce our latitude, the hour, and tomorrow's weather, I deduce something more important than all of those."
>
> "What, pray, is that, Holmes?"
>
> "Someone, Watson, has stolen our tent."

Ho ho. But let's quench our mirth by considering the terms they use. Watson is able to construe some features of the next day's weather from the conditions around them. He's able to deduce their latitude by observing the position of known points. From observation, he's able to deduce a time of day it cannot be later than. He deduces.

Holmes, on the other hand, observes there is no obstruction between the recumbent Watson and the celestial star-show, so he can deduce the canvas is missing, but he can only put forward a hypothesis as to the reason. There are several possible causes for the missing tent: it could have blown away; burnt to the ground around them; or even not have been erected at all in the first place. It may even be a false-flag operation by Holmes himself to vilify Moriarty. Holmes' answer may the most likely, but it can't be inevitably true or false. That means he hasn't deduced the answer.

Holmes, no matter what process Conan Doyle claimed for his famous creation, is not a master of deduction. Holmes is an exponent of observation, hypothesis and inference, which are features of abductive and inductive reasoning. Neither of these forms of reasoning are robust enough to provide a conclusion that's guaranteed to be logically true or valid.

Logic is a truth-preserving system of inference. That means if the premises in an argument are true, the conclusion inferred from them must also be true. Must – not may be – must.

In everyday speech, however, *deduce* is often used as a synonym for *conclude* or *decide*. That being so, we might be inclined to let Sherlock off the hook. But since he's such an insufferable know-it-all, let's hold him to account. Sherlock does not deduce in the strict sense.

The purpose of this book is to look at the essentials of deductive reasoning, and spoil a good joke. Our first task is to understand the yawning chasm between deduction and Sherlock's actual reasoning. But first...

WHY BOTHER WITH REASONING?

In a nutshell, it will distinguish you from the 99.9 per cent of people, including business managers, teachers, professionals and detectives, who have no idea how to make logical decisions. Yes, I'm really using an appeal to intellectual snobbery. Mea culpa. Here's a better reason:

> If you're already a respected professional or business manager, and steward of millions (perhaps tens or hundreds of millions!) of other people's piastres, not to mention the livelihood of many, many employees, and you're unable to think and reason logically, then you have no business taking the money they pay you.

There, I said it. Read that last paragraph again.

Being able to reason will help you deserve the salary you get, and get the salary you deserve. You'll become better at sifting through the tonnage of information that ends up on your plate every day, deciding what's right to act upon and making correct decisions.

The school subject *critical thinking* is the first and only introduction for many people to the notion of reasoning. But these courses are too broad-brush and mild for situations where money and livelihoods ride on the decisions you make. They tend to concentrate on informal reasoning and fallacies, those milky, dilute versions of logic. Of course, mathematicians and IT people learn about grown-up logic as part of their syllabus. But other people, unless they study subjects such as psychology or philosophy, they'll never again be taxed with logic and reasoning.

Beyond, in the big, exciting world of management, employers know that candidates with grand academic qualifications and splendid CVs are not guaranteed to have a lick of sense. They need people who can think and reason, so unsurprisingly they sit job candidates down and chuck a lot of tests at them. Some are psychometric tests that aim to find out about management and learning styles, for instance, while others test reasoning and comprehension. The ability to think ahead and foresee consequences is a highly desirable trait in managers. Some organisations actively test interviewees for their ability to think downstream. They're really testing the candidates' aptitude to make valid inferences.

If you apply for management consulting positions, you can expect tests that are a little more probing than the usual glorified IQ test. They'll examine your logical reasoning skills. Commonly, these tests ask you to identify valid arguments in syllogisms, or analyse the logic in a passage of prose, which can lead to a few problems.

Sometimes the *correct* answers are just wrong. The folks administering the tests simply read the answers they're given, or let software do the marking. Often, only the author of the original test understands the answers, and authors make mistakes. Hard to believe, but true. [1] Moreover, so much material is copied and re-used, the original author may be unknown

Furthermore, tests don't always make it clear whether they're testing abstract reasoning or practical judgement. Often, questions are made deliberately surreal to force candidates to focus on reasoning that goes against the grain of common sense, for example:

> If some humans are horses and all horses are fish, how many fish are humans? None, some or all?

---

[1] I completed reasoning tests at a management consultancy that contained an incorrect answer. "No-one ever gets that one right," the administrator told me.

Somewhere in there is a perfectly logical argument with an utterly mad-sounding answer. Other times, tests use nonsense terms to force you to reason, and not get distracted by meaning. So questions can read like this:

> If all Bloots are Chots and some Dips are not Chots, which of the following statements is correct?
>
> a) some Chots are not Dips
>
> b) some Bloots are not Dips
>
> c) some Dips are not Bloots

Worse, the vocabulary of reasoning uses a few words in a particular sense. *Some* means *one or more*, not *several*. Two statements linked by *or* can both be true. Unless the test-sitter is aware of the special meanings, he or she can only search for answers that sound likely, rather than deduce by logic.

All this being the case, it makes sense to try to understand the small number of valid arguments, and to be aware of the main formal fallacies reasoning is prone to. An understanding of how deductive reasoning works is a distinct advantage to the savvy candidate because most job applicants haven't a clue. When it comes to applying for a management role, there's no point dragging yourself down the level of your competitors.

Here's a disappointing reality: management is big on decisiveness, but awfully average at reasoning. If you're climbing the ladder of responsibility, among your colleagues you'll find some good thinkers and, without putting it too mildly, some idiots. They may have buckets of experience in operations or sales or finance, but that gives them no exemption from the deficiencies of reasoning we're all susceptible to. Whisper it: some of the idiots are already treading the soft carpets of the C-suite's lofty aerie.

Most corrosive of all are the managers believe their status itself confers magical powers of insight and understanding. If that were so, every organisation would be like an academy; mistakes would be unknown; all decisions would be tip-top; every venture would be a triumph; and every day at work would be like frolicking in the sun-dappled uplands of enlightenment. Alas, most managers use their instinct to make decisions and rationalise their choices afterwards. More often than not, they want to appear decisive, rather than find a true or valid answer.

If you bother to understand deductive reasoning you will be a smarter person and a better manager. Moreover, you'll stand out from the herd. Your ability to see through the fog of bogus reasoning and half-baked thinking will ensure your opinion is sought and valued. Let others accumulate years of experience learning from their mistakes. Your reasoning skills will let you walk into problems and cut through the competing claims of different opinions. And, best of all, you're going to be right.

THE BASIC PLOT

Once you understand reasoning and argument, you're going to notice nonsense everywhere. Much of it will be unintended; some will be deliberate misdirection. The worst chicanery will be people insisting that what they say is conclusive, and therefore backed up by those ruthless arbiters – reason, logic and deduction. It rarely will be.

You're going to spend a lot of time hearing other people talking through their hat. In meetings, around the office, at home, in class, at the gym, on TV, on the train, you're going to be surrounded by ostensibly smart people talking nonsense a fair amount of the time. How you choose to deal with that is up to you. Try not to become insufferably smug – it didn't work for me.

The problem people have is putting together a sound or valid *argument*. An argument is a connected series of statements intended to establish a position or a truth. It's a process of reasoning.

Yes, *argument* can also mean a good punch-up or, as we call it back in the land of my forefathers, a wedding. But in the world of reasoning, an argument is simply the case you put forward to explain why what you're saying is correct (or what the other person claims is wrong). Every time you find yourself saying:

I believe this because…, or

You're wrong because…

…you're engaged in an argument. When we try to persuade people, we use arguments. However, most people's arguments are unbelievably shallow. Most aren't arguments at all; they're perceptual biases, inclinations, ill-formed dispositions and temperament that, when articulated, can only form some semblance of reasoning if embellished with fallacies.

A fallacy is an error in reasoning that makes your argument wrong or weak. There are many informal fallacies, literally hundreds of them. They include basing your argument on some generalisation, false cause and effect, personal attacks and emotional appeals. This book concerns the logical fractures in deductive reasoning. There are fewer of them, but they can be tricky.

One phrase you should learn and repeat often, because it annoys people, is *non sequitur*. (Latin for *it does not follow*.)[2] In general, a non sequitur can be any random statement that doesn't seem to belong to the ones before it:

> Technical director: "The booster rocket has placed the satellite in a geostationary orbit."
>
> Intern: "Wallpaper paste tastes squidgy."

Specifically, in reasoning a non sequitur is a duff conclusion, something that isn't proven or supported by the statements in your argument. It's something that's not quite wrong enough to qualify as a formal fallacy. For instance:

> A company that makes computer games doubled its sales in three years, therefore twice as many people play computer games than three years ago.

The conclusion is a non sequitur. The statistic may happen to be true, but it's not supported by the evidence presented. First, one company's sales probably doesn't reflect the whole market – it may have launched an

---

[2] If some clever clogs maintains they know the Latin origins, be sure to comment further that the third conjugation passive voice reveals the verb *sequi* is a regular deponent verb – one which is passive in voice but active in meaning.

especially successful game. Or perhaps customers are buying twice as many games as before. Or the firm doubled the price of its products. Or there may actually be three times as many players in the market and the firm is falling behind its competitors. In reality, some combination of several reasons is likely.

Another word you'll see a lot in discussions about reasoning is *premise* (and its plural, unsurprisingly, *premises*). A premise is a statement, an assumption, that you use in an argument leading to a conclusion.

(Premise) All humans are mortal (true)

(Premise) All accountants are human (true)

(Conclusion) Ergo, all accountants are mortal (valid)

Here, both premises are true, and the reasoning used is logical. Therefore, the conclusion must be true, even if it resonates a lot less than "*all accountants must die*", which could easily be mistaken for a slogan or a to-do list.

The three-line argument:

A general statement or truth

Followed by specific statement or fact

Leading to a conclusion that must be true

... is called a categorical syllogism. Think of it as a limerick for logic. Categorical means the statements are unconditional, absolute, flat-out true assertions of fact. (Later we'll also see hypothetical syllogisms that contain conditions.) Syllogisms are the neatest, most succinct way of expressing deductive reasoning.

The first statement is called the *major premise*. It sets the scene. The second is the *minor premise*. It sets out a specific instance of the major premise. When the major and minor premises are dovetailed together, they lead to a conclusion that must be true:

Major premise: to be legal, car tyres must have tread 1.6mm deep across ¾ of the width of the tyre

Minor premise: my car tyre is as smooth as Michelangelo's David's bum

Conclusion: Therefore, my tyre is not legal.

Moving on, the words *infer* and *imply* crop up a lot, so it's important to understand the difference.

Infer means to construe, deduce, conclude from information or premises. Infer is something the person receiving information does:

The teacher explains that some mammals are dogs, and some mammals are cats. The pupils infer that mammals are animals, not trees or spaceships.

Imply, by contrast, is what the giver of information does. It means literally to enfold; figuratively, to express indirectly, insinuate, hint, or suggest:

The CEO refrained from directly criticising politicians, but his repeated use of the phrase *firing squad* implied a profound dislike of them.

With those basics in place, it's time to take off our socks and shoes and wade in a little bit.

THE THREE MAIN CHARACTERS

Although the main topic for this book is deductive reasoning, it's important to understand the dramatis personae of the whole play. The three main kinds of reasoning frameworks are: **induction**, **abduction** and **deduction**. For the purpose of comparing them, we can say they all hang together using three components:

- a **precondition** – a prior fact, event or circumstance that triggers the reasoning, and

- a **general rule** whereby the precondition implies the conclusion, and

- a **conclusion** or outcome that ensues when the precondition and general rule operate.

So let's canter through each type of reasoning, and see how the different kinds of logic work:

Induction: The pavement becomes slippery [outcome] whenever it has snowed [prior event]. Therefore, when it snows, the pavement becomes slippery [general rule].

Abduction: The pavement is slippery now [outcome]. When it snows, the pavement becomes slippery [general rule]. Therefore, it must have snowed [prior event].

Deduction: When it snows, the pavement gets slippery [general rule]. It has been snowing [prior event]. Therefore, the pavement is slippery [outcome].

Each kind of reasoning derives a different component in the argument. But only the deductive argument, if its premises (rule and precondition) are true, guarantees to supply a true and valid conclusion.

In real life, all three kinds are used in a blend of techniques just as red, yellow and blue are blended to make the full gamut of colours. Every endeavour demands some element from all reasoning kinds. It's important to keep in mind what we're searching for: some rule, precondition or conclusion.

Inductive reasoning – an outline

Inductive reasoning proceeds from a specific observation to a broad generalisation.

In the example:

The pavement becomes slippery [outcome] whenever it has snowed [prior event]. Therefore, when it snows, the pavement becomes slippery [general rule].

We see induction reaches a broad generalisation from observations about snowfall and slipperiness. If the pavement happens to be slippery, we can infer snowfall as the probable cause because we know that snowfall entails slipperiness.

A strong induction allows a pattern to build, then derives a rule. The strong induction is valid. It says: every instance so far follows this pattern, so this pattern is a valid basis of inference. In formula terms, it looks like this:

Formula	Example
$A1 = B1$	The first T-shirt I pull from the washing machine is pink
$A2 = B2$	The second T-shirt is pink
$A_n = B_n$	All the T-shirts so far are pink
Therefore, all $A = B$	Therefore, all the T-shirts are pink

That's a *strong* induction, based on all the evidence so far. But it doesn't have to be true. By contrast, a *weak* induction would reach an importantly different conclusion:

| Therefore, the next A must = B | The next T-shirt must be pink |

This weak induction is in fact an *unwarranted deduction*. It says:

I deduce that the next T-shirt must be pink

... which is something we're not able to do. We can't be certain what colour the next T-shirt will be. All we know, with a sinking heart, is that before we empty the machine we'll find the red T-shirt with non-colour-fast dye.

Inductive reasoning is the thinking we use in everyday life to make our point. It's at the heart of conversation, complaints, news editorials, opinions, arguments and so on. We state what we've seen happening, then offer an opinion based on our personal experience or belief of those events (our own personal rule).

Most of the mistakes we make are hasty or faulty generalisations. Inductive reasoning is why. It does produce a generalised sort of truth, but we're not always good at determining exactly what that general rule is.

Inductive reasoning is referred to as informal: it doesn't use a specific vocabulary or structure. As arguments go, it wears jeans and a T-shirt and drinks beer from a can. It doesn't employ the rigid logic of formal deduction. It uses no magnifying glasses. The very softness of the inductive playing field means arguments are subject to hundreds of non-sequiturs that weaken them. Among such fallacies are faulty or hasty generalisation, appeals to emotion, wrong cause and correlation inferences, red herring arguments, personal attacks, and shifting the burden of proof.

Here's a kind of argument you hear every day:

The council shouldn't give planning permission for new houses to be built [conclusion]. If it does allow itself to be persuaded by the promise of extra tax revenues and grant planning permission [precondition], there'll soon be housing estates covering all the fields [questionable general rule].

This is a *slippery slope argument.* It argues that some present action is wrong or bad because it might lead to worse outcomes later. This result may turn out to be true but, here, over-development is hypothetical. Hypothetical things are not deductively certain. So the slippery slope is a weak argument, but it's one we hear every day. Slow progression is precisely how things do evolve.

A much stronger argument would be unsuitability of the development for the neighbourhood, some loss of amenity to residents, or that the site is unsuitable for development:

The council shouldn't give planning permission for new houses [desired conclusion]. The site is a flood plain by a river [precondition], so it's likely to flood at the drop of a hat [general rule].

Errors in inductive reasoning lead to the kind of woolly, everyday thinking that gets us into trouble most of the time. When there's no unarguable fact, we use opinions, myths, 'common' knowledge, bias, generalisations, prejudice, and so on, to validate what we claim to be true or real.

We like to pretend that our opinions are reasoned and based on firm ground. But usually we reach our conclusion (express an opinion, assert a fact, and so on) that we like, then use any kind of reasoning to justify it. That muddled thinking is called *confirmation bias* and *ex post facto rationalisation.* It's probably why we get things so wrong much of the time.

Inductive reasoning is called a bottom-up approach because it starts with specific observations and advances towards an abstract or general theory.

Abductive reasoning – an outline

Abductive reasoning proceeds from observation and general principle to form a best-shot explanation for the observation.

Abduction lets us generate hypotheses and look for the best account for specific events and observations. It's the thinking used in enquiry and research. We start with observations, then apply whatever rules seem to fit best. We then infer a precondition – a cause – that could account for the conclusion. Here's the example again:

> The pavement is slippery now [outcome]. When it snows, the pavement becomes slippery [general rule]. Therefore, it must have snowed [prior event].

Usually we begin with an incomplete set of observations, and head towards the best-fit hypothesis for them. Here, we're able to infer snowfall as an explanation for the slipperiness. We know this is the most probable explanation since our general rule says that snowfall entails slipperiness. As a result, abduction generates a best guess, best-fit conclusion.

> My car has ground to a halt. If a car grinds to a halt, most commonly it's run out of fuel. Therefore, the most likely explanation is my car ran out of fuel

This makes good sense in an abductive context, but it's deductively invalid. In the example, there are several possible causes for a car conking out besides fuel, such as an electronic control unit giving up the ghost, a fuel pump, a defunct alternator, and so on.

So, abductive reasoning asks: if this is the effect, what was the cause and how did it lead to this result? There always remains some uncertainty because abductive conclusions can only be the best available answer at the time. Further observation and evidence may later change the conclusion, so abductive conclusions are necessarily provisional. This form of reasoning is important in diagnostic enquiries, crime detection, as well as scientific theories.

By the way, a *scientific theory* is not the same as a good guess. It's a strongly corroborated explanation, arrived at by using scientific method, tested and confirmed in experiments and observations. Within abductive reasoning, we'll find inductive processes and deductions being made. But the overall abductive line of enquiry moves from observation to a theory that best accounts for the observation. More examples:

> A doctor learns that a patient is experiencing pain and stiffness in a joint. X-rays show wear and tear in the joint. She diagnoses osteoarthritis as the best explanation.

> A juror hears evidence against a defendant. He isn't entirely certain the defendant is guilty, but thinks the defendant's criminality is more likely than any other explanation.

And who better to consult than Sherlock?

> Street urchin Wiggins emerges from my kitchen with jam and sugar smeared all around his chops. Going in, I see the box of doughnuts I bought has several missing. I didn't see Wiggins actually eating them, but there's no-one else in the kitchen, and there's evidence plastered all over Wiggins' smug and grubby dial. The facts may be inconclusive, but it's safe enough for me to decide beyond reasonable doubt that Wiggins is a thieving tyke.

Sherlock might claim: *"I deduce the little monster is the thief."* He does nothing of the sort. He abduces it. (*Abduce* is the verb form of abduction in this context; *to abduct* is more of a people thing.)

Conan Doyle's Sherlock Holmes often tells Watson of the need to reason backwards from effects to causes. This is abductive reasoning, and it gives Sherlock no grounds whatsoever for the dismissive certainty of his conclusions.

Deductive reasoning – an outline

Deduction is to reach a conclusion, starting with a general statement, and applying a specific instance of that statement or rule:

> When it snows, the pavement gets slippery [general rule]. It has been snowing [prior event]. Therefore, the pavement is slippery [outcome].

In deductive reasoning, we're able to derive a conclusion about the state of the pavement having identified an appropriate general rule and narrowed down the circumstances that apply to that rule. If those premises are true, deduction guarantees that the conclusion is true or valid. In effect, our example can be re-cast like this:

> If it has been snowing, then the pavement gets slippery
>
> It has been snowing
>
> Therefore, the pavement is slippery

It's one of the more common forms of deduction. The reasoning follows a sure and certain path:

Reasoning	Example
If P, then Q	If I have the right password, then I can log on as the financial director
P is true	Yes, I have the right password
Therefore, Q is true	Therefore, I can log on as the financial director

Hello, Hawaii! This form of logic is called *affirming the antecedent* or *modus ponens*. It's a valid form of deduction. Deduction is the only form of reasoning that guarantees the truth of its conclusions, if the premises are true. That makes deduction a valuable tool, one that needs a little more care to get right. To safeguard its clarity, deductive logic is unforgiving and rigorous. It's fussy. It doesn't allow practitioners to dial in their thinking and try to fuzzy it through. As you'd expect, mathematics is the apex of deductive reasoning. For instance:

If $x = 2$, and $y = 3$

Then $2x + 3y = 13$

The premises absolutely guarantee the conclusion, no argument. It's this level of precision that makes deductive reasoning the gold standard by which we measure less precise and rigorous methods.

Note that the propositional variables used in the formula are **P** and **Q** as is customary, just as **x** and **y** are mathematical variables. P and Q are true or false, rather than numerical values.

And if we're being picky, we should say that a deductive inference only professes to guarantee the conclusion. It's possible to make a false deductive inference, and it's possible for the premises used to be disconnected. If, for example, we said:

When it snows, the flowers come into bloom. It is snowing. Therefore it's Thursday.

Nothing but non sequiturs there. The rule is wrong; the conclusion is, frankly, bizarre. Just because something has the appearance of deductive reasoning, it ain't necessarily so.

OUR NEW BEST FRIEND

So, the most sure-footed form of reasoning is deductive. It's the gold standard. Think of it as a formal process wearing a dark suit, sober tie and hand-made shoes. Perhaps a cape. No deerstalker. Deductive reasoning leads to specific conclusions, incontestable, must-be-true answers. For example:

All dogs bark (true)

All labradoodles are dogs (true)

Therefore, all labradoodles bark (valid)

The conclusion is valid, even if it's less germane than *"My neighbour's dog is a flaming nuisance."*

Mathematics is governed by formal logic, as are philosophy, science generally, programming and other topics that demand a lot of brain meat. Deductive reasoning has an ideal expression, our new best friend – the categorical syllogism. Categorical means a statement of fact – it's not conditional or hypothetical. A syllogism is an argument in which we deduce a conclusion from the two premises. This is one of the most common forms:

A = B

C = A

Therefore, C = B

Nothing scary at all. Here's how it looks with some flesh on the bones:

All noble gases (A) are (=) stable (B)

Helium (C) is (=) a noble gas (A)

Therefore, helium (C) is (=) stable (B)

Another example, this time using an equivalent statement:

Angles less than 90 degrees are acute angles

This angle is 45 degrees

Therefore, this is an acute angle

A syllogism contains three propositions – two premises and a conclusion. It usually opens with a general statement or truth called a **major premise**. That's followed by a specific instance called the **minor premise**. The final part is the **conclusion**. Sometimes the major and minor premises get swapped, but it's better to be consistent and use the major premise first. It also feels more natural.

Premises	Example
A = B (major premise)	All thieves (A) are (=) criminals (B) (general)
C = A (minor premise)	Moriarty (C) is (=) a thief (A) (specific)
Therefore, C = B (conclusion)	Therefore, Moriarty (C) is (=) a criminal (B)

From this logical structure, we can formulate almost all arguments that can give a true conclusion. The steeliest arguments use categorical propositions. These are statements that purport to be flat-out true. From them we can derive deducible[3] truths.

---

[3] *Deducible* is the correct adjective in this context. *Deductible* is when the tax people let you keep more of your own money and make out they're being generous.

A categorical proposition is just a sentence that asserts a true or valid argument. If we break down the sentence, we find two essential common components – a subject and a predicate – plus a quantifier. Let's start with quantifiers.

Quantifiers

A quantifier tells us which members of a class the premise applies to. Categorical syllogisms use four quantifiers. Each creates a different type of argument. The four quantifiers are:

- All
- No
- Some
- Some Are Not

Other expressions slot into one of these. For instance, *every* and *each* belong in **All**; *several* or *various* go in **Some**. *Some* just means *one or more*: it's not a specific amount. It's not **No** and it's not **All**.

The four quantifiers produce four types of argument called type **A**, type **E**, type **I**, and type **O**.

Quantifier	Argument
All … are	type A
No … are	type E
Some … are	type I
Some … are not	type O

The quantifiers are used like this:

Type A – All public houses sell beer

22

Type E – No sharks hang wallpaper

Type I – Some flowers give a scent at night-time

Type O – Some pop stars cannot sing in tune

It can help follow the reasoning if you mentally re-state the premises using the verb *to be*:

Type A – All public houses sell beer = **All** public houses **are** places that sell beer

Type E – No sharks hang wallpaper = **No** sharks **are** decorators who hang wallpaper

Type I – Some flowers give a scent at night-time = **Some** flowers **are** plants that give a scent at night-time

Type O – Some pop stars cannot sing in tune = **Some** pop stars **are not** people who can sing in tune

The quantifiers determine the type of argument that follows. Later we'll see how those four types combine to form valid or invalid arguments.

Subject and predicate

At its simplest, each proposition has two terms. Like normal sentences, propositions divide into subject and predicate. The subject is the noun, pronoun or phrase that governs the verb in the premise. The predicate is the rest of the sentence. All three parts of a syllogism have a subject and predicate.

Important: when referring to the structure of a syllogism, the terms subject and predicate *always* refer to those parts in the conclusion. Yes, both major and minor premises grammatically have a subject and predicate, but it's the conclusion that we're interested in. Conclusions of each argument type might look like this:

Therefore, **all** cats (Subject) throw up on the rug (Predicate)

Therefore, **no** cats (Subject) clean up after themselves (Predicate)

Therefore, **some** owners (Subject) use cheap cleaning products (Predicate)

Therefore, **some** cheap cleaning products (Subject) **are not** effective (Predicate)

All conclusions have the sentence order: subject then predicate.

Major term, minor term, middle term

A quick recap: a categorical syllogism features two premises and a conclusion. It usually opens with a general statement or truth called a major premise, followed by a specific instance called the minor premise. The final part is the conclusion.

Again, the major and minor premises are sometimes swapped around. For consistency, it's best always to put the major premise first. We've already seen major and minor premises, but it doesn't hurt to look another example:

A = B (major premise)	All fish live in water
C = A (minor premise)	All sharks are fish
Therefore, C = B (conclusion)	Therefore, all sharks live in water

Within the syllogism are three components, each of which appears twice: a **major term**, **minor term** and a **middle term**.

The major term is the part of the major premise that appears as the predicate in the conclusion – the letter B in the example:

A = **B** (major term)	All fish **live in water**
C = A	All sharks are fish
Therefore, C = **B** (major term)	Therefore, all sharks **live in water**

The minor term is the is the part of the minor premise that appears as the subject in the conclusion – the letter C in the example:

A = B	All fish live in water
C (minor term) = A	**All sharks** are fish
Therefore, **C** (minor term) = B	Therefore, **all sharks** live in water

The final term appears both in the major and minor premises, but not the conclusion. This is the middle term. The major and minor premises are linked by the middle term. The link gives logical backbone to the syllogism. In this example, *fish* links *living in water* and *sharks* like a stepping stone between them. This middle term enables us to draw a conclusion about *sharks* and *living in water*.

A (middle term) = B	All **fish** live in water
C = **A** (middle term)	All sharks are **fish**
Therefore, C = B	Therefore, all sharks live in water

These components are important. In order to reach a deductively true or valid conclusion, we have to be rigorous in setting arguments out accurately. Many of the formal errors in deductive reasoning stem from an deficiency in one or more of the terms.

Before we move on, pay attention to the position of the middle term in both the major and minor premise. It can appear in two places (subject or predicate) in two premises. That means there are four possible configurations or arrangements for the middle term. These are called figures. The four figures of syllogisms have an important role in shaping the arguments they present.

The sign of four

So far, to keep things simple and consistent, I've used the structure known as a Figure 1 syllogism to demonstrate the logic of arguments. In fact, there are four arrangements.

As long as a syllogism features a middle term in both the major and minor terms, the structure of the argument is solid. The middle term can hop around a bit, appearing in the first or second part of the major and minor terms. That means the middle term can appear in any one of four configurations called *figures*. This means that syllogisms come in four figures. But only the middle term moves around within the different figures. Note that in each figure:

- the conclusion is always the same: that is, subject then predicate.
- the predicate of the conclusion always appears in the major premise.
- the subject of the conclusion always appears in the minor premise.
- the only change is the position of the middle term in both major and minor premises.
- subject and predicate refer to how the terms appear in the conclusion.

Here are the four figures of categorical syllogisms with the different positions the important terms appear in:

Figure 1 syllogism

Major premise =	**Middle term**	then	Predicate
Minor premise =	Subject	then	**Middle term**
Conclusion =	Subject	then	Predicate

Figure 2 syllogism

Major premise =	Predicate	then	**Middle term**
Minor premise =	Subject	then	**Middle term**
Conclusion =	Subject	then	Predicate

Figure 3 syllogism

Major premise =	**Middle term**	then	Predicate
Minor premise =	**Middle term**	then	Subject
Conclusion =	Subject	then	Predicate

Figure 4 syllogism

Major premise =	Predicate	then	**Middle term**
Minor premise =	**Middle term**	then	Subject
Conclusion =	Subject	then	Predicate

The 'shape' of the arguments in each figure changes. You should recognise figure 1 right away, because that's the figure used in all the examples so far.

Each figure is as logically robust as the others. The 'chosen' figure forms itself around the argument we present. We don't need to massage arguments to fit any particular figure. Precisely expressed major and minor premises will produce a syllogism in one of the four figures available.

Again, note the positions of the middle terms, shown in bold and underlined:

Figure 1	Figure 2	Figure 3	Figure 4
A = B	A = **B**	**A** = B	A = **B**
C = **A**	C = **B**	**A** = C	**B** = C
Therefore, C = B	Therefore, C = A	Therefore, C = B	Therefore, C = A

Shorthand for syllogisms

Again, a quick recap to ensure the basics are clear. Every proposition in a categorical syllogism contains a quantifier: *All*, *No*, *Some* are and *Some are not*. These determine the type of argument, which are referred to as **A**, **E**, **I** and **O**.

All =	type **A**
No =	type **E**
Some are =	type **I**
Some are not =	type **O**

In order to keep track of the many possible syllogisms, valid and otherwise, a system of shorthand has been devised. A complete categorical syllogism can be summed up by the argument type for each of the three propositions, followed by its figure number.

For example, a syllogism using a Some, All and a Some argument and with middle terms configured as **Figure 4** is described as **I A I – 4**:

Some foods (predicate) are oranges (middle)

All oranges (middle) are fruits (subject)

Therefore, some fruits (subject) are foods (predicate)

Remember the odd example earlier? It's a **figure 2** syllogism, with Chots being the middle term.

All Bloots are Chots

Some Dips are not Chots:

Therefore, some Dips are not Bloots

The correct answer to the question is c). This syllogism can be expressed as **A O O – 2**. The other surreal example was:

Some humans are horses

All horses are fish

Therefore, some fish are humans

The answer to the question is some, and it's an **I A I – 4** syllogism. While it's a logical argument, it's still a perfectly mad answer.

By the way, standard mnemonics have been used to remember the configuration of valid syllogisms. The mnemonics are words whose vowels match the argument types – **A**, **E**, **I** and **O** – in the correct order. They sound like minor characters in some obscure Grand Guignol play.

For example, the first, **A A A – 1**, is **Barbara**. Later comes **E I O – 3**, **Ferison**. And last of all is **I A I – 4**, **Dimatis**. In all, there are 24 mnemonics. They've been used for centuries, but I'm not convinced they help very much. I include them only in case you use another book or website discussing this topic, as a way of cross-referencing different sources.

I don't recommend you begin a discussion in your favourite pub or bar:

"Who else thinks the existential fallacy in a Fesapo syllogism is a nit-picky construct and not really a thing?"

Because welcome to Lonely City. Population: you.

Of the 256 possible combinations, only 24 categorical syllogisms can ever produce a valid argument, so it's easier to list all the possible valid ones than wade through all the duff versions.

Even so, nine of these ostensibly valid cases are questionable – they potentially commit an *existential fallacy* by referring to an empty category. These are conclusions that are logically valid, but unlikely to have many instances in real life, or to offer strange implications. We'll see examples of what that means as we go along, and the section Formal Fallacies in Syllogisms covers existential fallacies in some detail.

That leaves just 15 common, unquestionably valid syllogisms. To make things simple, I've listed all 24 syllogisms, from figures 1 to 4, and in the alphabetical order of their argument types, starting with everyone's favourite, the evergreen, basic **A A A – 1**.

Valid figure 1 syllogisms

Major premise =	Middle term	then	Predicate
Minor premise =	Subject	then	Middle term
Conclusion =	Subject	then	Predicate

1. **A A A – 1 – Barbara**

All cats are carnivores

All tigers are cats

Therefore, all tigers are carnivores

2. A A I – 1 – Barbari (possible existential fallacy)

All humans are mortal

All women are humans

Therefore, some women are mortal [some are immortal?]

3. A I I – 1 – Darii

All birds have feathers

Some pets are birds

Therefore, some pets have feathers

4. E A E – 1 – Celarent

No aeroplanes are submarines

All Jumbo Jets are aeroplanes

Therefore, no Jumbo Jets are submarines

5. E A O – 1 – Celaront (possible existential fallacy)

No fish are feathered

All salmon are fish

Therefore, some salmon are not feathered [some are?]

6. E I O – 1 – Ferio

No homework is enjoyable

Some school activity is homework

Therefore, some school activity is not enjoyable

Valid figure 2 syllogisms

Major premise =	Predicate	then	Middle term
Minor premise =	Subject	then	Middle term
Conclusion =	Subject	then	Predicate

7. A E E – 2 – Camestres

All spaceships are vehicles

No mountains are vehicles

Therefore, no mountains are spaceships

8. A E O – 2 – Camestros (possible existential fallacy)

All clowns wear bright clothes

No funeral directors wear bright clothes

Therefore, some funeral directors are not clowns [some are?]

9. A O O – 2 – Baroco

All taxes are state-run rackets

Some payments are not state-run rackets

Therefore, some payments are not taxes

10. E A E – 2 – Cesare

No walls are entrances

All doors are entrances

Therefore, no doors are walls

11. E A O – 2 – Cesaro (possible existential fallacy)

No rabbits are primates

All monkeys are primates

Therefore, some monkeys are not rabbits [some are?]

12. E I O – 2 – Festino

No websites are magazines

Some TV listings are magazines

Therefore, some TV listings are not websites

Valid figure 3 syllogisms

Major premise =	Middle term	then	Predicate
Minor premise =	Middle term	then	Subject
Conclusion =	Subject	then	Predicate

13. A A I – 3 – Darapti (possible existential fallacy)

All pubs are licensed premises

All pubs are vendors of beer

Therefore, some vendors of beer are licensed premises [no other kind should exist]

14. A I I – 3 – Datisi

All people are imperfect

Some people are saintly

Therefore, some saintly people are imperfect

15. E A O – 3 – Felapton (possible existential fallacy)

No rap music is tuneful

All rap music is bad language

Therefore, some bad language is not tuneful [some is?]

16. E I O – 3 – Ferison

No dogs are dolphins

Some dogs are strong swimmers

Therefore, some strong swimmers are not dolphins

17. I A I – 3 – Disamis

Some vehicles are fast

All vehicles consume fuel

Therefore, some fuel-consuming things are fast

18. O A O – 3 – Bocardo

Some examples are not correct

All examples are illustrations

Therefore, some illustrations are not correct

Valid figure 4 syllogisms

Major premise =	Predicate	then	Middle term
Minor premise =	Middle term	then	Subject
Conclusion =	Subject	then	Predicate

19. A A I – 4 – Bramantip (possible existential fallacy)

All landmines are lethal

All lethal things are to be avoided

Therefore, some things to be avoided are landmines [some things not to be avoided are landmines?]

20. A E E – 4 – Calenes

All poisons are harmful

No harmful things are healthy

Therefore, no healthy things are poisons

21. A E O – 4 – Calemos (possible existential fallacy)

All roses are plants

No plants are animals

Therefore, some animals are not roses [some are?]

22. E A O – 4 – Fesapo (possible existential fallacy)

No liquids are solids

All solids are things with mass

Therefore, some things with mass are not liquids

23. E I O – 4 – Fresison

No peninsulas are islands

Some islands are countries

Therefore, some countries are not peninsulas

24. I A I – 4 – Dimatis

Some future CEOs are students of logic

All students of logic are intelligent people

Therefore, some intelligent people are future CEOs

That's it, folks. The sum total of all possible, valid, deductive arguments.

For the record, there's just one argument that's unquestionably valid in all four figures. It's like O-negative blood, the universal donor of the syllogism world. It's **E I O**: *No*, *Some*, *Some are not*.

In addition, there's one argument that's valid in all four figures, but also subject to a possible existential fallacy in all four figures too. It's **E A O**: *No, All, Some are not.*

A HANDY CRIB SHEET

Here's a summary of all valid syllogisms. Technically, having a copy or a photo of this page in a test would be against the spirit of the exercise. But if it's a recruitment test, they started it.

- Identify the three-letter summary of the three propositions in your syllogism. For example, **E A O**. Again:

All = A, No = E, Some are = I, Some are not = O

- Identify the figure of the syllogism. Find the common term in the major and minor premises. This is the middle term. Find the middle terms, then see which figure you're dealing with:

Figure	1	2	3	4
Major	**Mid +** Pred	Pred + **Mid**	**Mid +** Pred	Pred + **Mid**
Minor	Sub + **Mid**	Sub + **Mid**	**Mid +** Sub	**Mid +** Sub
Conclusion	Sub + Pred	Sub + Pred	Sub + Pred	Sub + Pred

- Check the arguments under the correct figure below. If your syllogism isn't listed here, it's not valid. Also, syllogisms marked with asterisks ** signify a possible existential fallacy.

Figure	1	2	3	4
Valid Arguments	A A A	A E E	A A I **	A A I **
	A A I **	A E O **	A I I	A E E
	A I I	A O O	E A O **	A E O **
	E A E	E A E	E I O	E A O **
	E A O **	E A O **	I A I	E I O
	E I O	E I O	O A O	I A I

Why nine out of ten syllogisms don't work

If there are 256 syllogism combinations and only 24 can be valid, what happened to the rest? The answer is they suffer from one of the formal fallacies that invalidate the argument. We've looked at all the valid versions, so you don't need to know the formal fallacies in order to work out what's not valid. But knowing the rules will help you understand how the mechanics of syllogisms work and why so many were casualties.

Formal fallacies don't consider the sense of an argument, only whether its form is valid. When arguments have a mistake in their logical structure they must be invalid, even if the premises sometimes appear to be true and the meaning makes sense.

For instance:

Some creatures with wings can fly

All ostriches are creatures with wings

Therefore, some ostriches can fly (invalid)

At first glance, the argument looks promising, but the conclusion is false. In fact, we can see it's an **I A I – 1** syllogism. It doesn't appear in our list of valid Figure 1 syllogisms. That means this form of syllogism can never produce a valid conclusion. What about:

All creatures that fly have wings

No ostriches can fly

Therefore, no ostriches have wings (invalid)

No, still wrong. The reason ostriches can't fly is not because they lack wings. The problem here is an unstated assumption that all creatures with wings must be able to fly, which is a false premise. This time the structure is **A E E – 1**. Again it doesn't show up in the list of valid syllogisms.

In order to understand why reasoning that looks right turns out to be wrong, we'll look at the different types of fallacy. We saw earlier that some valid arguments can have an existential fallacy. This is a quantification fallacy – it revolves around the quantifiers **All**, **No**, **Some**, **Some are not** – while the others are formal syllogistic fallacies.

Existential fallacy

If there weren't a fallacy called *existential* we'd have to make one up. *Existential* is the word that makes you sound smart, as if you wander around Lidl quoting Sartre and dissing Spinoza.

In the list of valid syllogisms we came across nine that might have problems with an existential fallacy. We saw that it's possible to construct a syllogism that with resounding logic reaches a conclusion that's complete nonsense. It implies a class of things exists, when we know for sure it probably doesn't (or shouldn't) – an empty class. Here's an example showing why certain syllogisms can be fallacious.

It's an **A A I – 1** argument, which we've already seen is susceptible to an existentialist fallacy.

The explanation involves two new terms: *universal propositions* and *particular statements*. An example first:

All geese are waterfowl [universal proposition]

All ganders are geese [universal proposition]

Therefore, some ganders are waterfowl [particular statement – are some not?]

The existential fallacy applies here because saying some ganders are waterfowl implies that some of them must not be. That can't be right. So how did we get there?

Sweeping **All** or **No** statements – are called *universal propositions* since they apply to every member of the class of things they refer to. But they offer no assurance that the things they talk about actually exist. Perhaps they do; perhaps they don't. The premise doesn't care. From the point of view of reasoning, therefore, universal statements – affirmative or negative – do not have what is called *existential import.*

All leprechauns live in Ireland

No unicorns live in Essex

All Martians like mashed potato

See? Universal statements don't imply their subjects exist, even if they do make you sound like you need stronger medication. Even universal statements that appear as conclusions still carry no existential import.

By contrast, **Some** or **Some are not** conclusions are not universal, it's a *particular statement.* Only some members of the class have the quality referred to. It's as if someone went through every member of the class and checked to see if each had the quality or not. Those found to have the requisite quality would actually have to exist in order to be matched. Particular statements, therefore, do imply that the thing they talk about exists. In other words, particular statements do have *existential import.* This is how the four different arguments convey existential import:

Type A – All A are B	universal affirmative = no existential import
Type E – No A are B	universal negative = no existential import
Type I – Some A are B	particular affirmative= existential import
Type O – Some A are not B	particular negative= existential import

A syllogism that suffers from an existential fallacy might look like this. It's an **A A I – 1** format, the first valid one that's listed, but susceptible to an existential fallacy:

All leprechauns live in Ireland [no existential import]

All people called Zebedee are leprechauns [no existential import]

Therefore, some people called Zebedee live in Ireland [yes, a particular statement]

Here we have a conclusion that some people called Zebedee live in Ireland. Such a conclusion is particular, and it implies the existence of Ireland-based Zebedees. However, it also implies that some leprechauns called Zebedee do not live in Ireland, which the major premise doesn't allow for.

When it crops up, an existential fallacy occurs because the conclusion contains more information – the existential import, the promise, if you like, that there truly are some examples of the thing promised – than its premises supply. It is therefore invalid.

In a nutshell, universal premises leading to a particular conclusion suffer from the existential fallacy. As universal and particular premises are determined by their quantifier, the existential fallacy is classed as a quantification fallacy.

As with many things involving profound cogitation, there are differing opinions among experts. Some argue that affirmative statements (types **A** and **I**) do imply existence, while negative ones (types **E** and **O**) do not. You could also argue that any proposition may or may not imply the existence of something, depending on the individual statement and what it's asserting. In this section, however, I've preferred the version that is, I believe, most widely accepted.

> Rule: A syllogism that has two universal premises (types A or E) cannot have a particular conclusion (types I and O). If it does it will encounter an existential fallacy.

Four terms – fallacy

A categorical syllogism has to contain three unambiguous terms. Remember this figure 1 structure?

A = B

C = A

Therefore, C = B

If the syllogism does not have exactly three terms, it's invalid. With fewer than three terms, we couldn't follow a path through the arguments and reach any kind of conclusion.

If there are more than three, the reasoning falls on its nose. There's no room for a "D" in a syllogism.

All cars (A) have wheels (B)

All tyres (C) have valves (D)

Therefore, … (nothing springs to mind)

So, if we try to shoehorn a fourth term into the argument, the syllogism wanders off into oblivion. Sometimes we see an argument that seems to have three terms, but it's an illusion.

Nothing is better than a loving family

Half a loaf is better than nothing

Therefore, half a loaf is better than a loving family (invalid)

Ho, ho. There are four terms because "nothing is better" and "better than nothing" mean two different things. The fourth term is caused by equivocation – a word or phrase that has two different meanings. The terms here are:

Nothing is better, loving family, half a loaf, better than nothing

Like trimesters at college, three terms is plenty. We need exactly three terms in three propositions for a valid syllogism.

Rule: A syllogism must have exactly three terms. No more. If we break this rule, we run into the fallacy of four terms.

Undistributed middle– fallacy

This sounds like a diet problem: "Why do I look as if I have everybody else's middle?" It's a formal fallacy that's quite straightforward once you get behind the jargon.

Remember the basic structure of a syllogism. Both premises contribute one term each to the conclusion, which I have underlined to save wear and tear on your eyeballs in this **A A A – 1** syllogism:

All thieves (middle term) are criminals (major term)

All embezzlers (minor term) are thieves (middle term)

Therefore, all embezzlers (minor term) are criminals (major term)]

The middle term thieves links the two premises and provides the logical rigour to the argument. It's the stepping stone between criminals and embezzlers that allows us to infer something from one about the other. To link the premises firmly, the middle term must be distributed in at least one of the premises.

At this point, let's take a short break to become familiar with distribution in deductive reasoning. It's relevant not just to the middle term, but to the next two sections on illicit majors and minors.

'Distributed' has a particular meaning

Distributed means the premises must account for all members of the class of things described by the term. They must all be affected or included. If the syllogism doesn't offer information about the whole class of the middle term, it can't make a robust connection between the major and minor premises. It's like this:

All golfers use golf clubs

Imagine that to make this categorical statement (knowing it to be true), we'd have to check the golf bag of every player on the first tee of every course in the world. We'd find at least one suitable smacking-shaped thing on the end of a stick, so the premise would be true. Thus, when we say all golfers do this, we have accounted for every member of the class of golfers. We're in a position to make a categorical statement about golfers' tools which must be true. When a premise says something about all members of a class of things, it is said to be distributed. Here, golfers is distributed.

Each type of argument – **All, No, Some, Some are not** – offers a different situation, but the question remains the same:

Have we accounted for them all?

To make a valid argument, the middle term must be distributed in either the major or minor premise. The middle term lies in both premises, and both premises have two parts – a subject and predicate. That means the middle term can be the subject or predicate in any one of the four types of argument. To see if the middle term is distributed, we need to check each argument type, looking at both the subject and predicate of those premises. First, type **A** arguments:

All golfers use golf clubs

To play the game, every golfer needs at least one club, therefore every member of the class of golfers is accounted for.

So the subject all golfers is distributed.

What about the predicate, the golf clubs? It's fair to assume some are possessed by non-players, shops, museums, gangsters, fairway-side rough, canals and storage lockers, as well as golfers. Only some of the world's supply of golf clubs are possessed by golfers. *Some* is a clue. We have only accounted for the clubs in the possession of actual golfers. The premise doesn't account for all members of the class.

So the predicate golf clubs is not distributed.

We continue the process with the next type **E:**

No swimmer wears a suit of armour

To be sure our statement is categorically true, we'd have to check every swimmer for a metal exterior. Every member of the class swimmers is included, as was the case with *all golfers*.

Therefore, the subject *no swimmer* is distributed.

For the premise to be true, we must sure all suits of armour were empty of swimmers. We could logically say "all suits of armour are not worn by swimmers". That means all members of the class suits of armour are accounted for.

Therefore, the predicate *suit of armour* is distributed.

The third type of argument is type **I**:

Some chief executives are hideously overpaid

For a **Some** statement to be true, we just have to find one example of overpay and one case of fair pay (to make sure we're not talking about **All** or **No** chief executives). As soon as we have one of each, we can stop looking. Not all chief executives are affected by the proposition. The clue was in the word *some*.

Therefore, the subject *some chief executives* is not distributed.

The class of hideously overpaid is not fully accounted for either. We stopped checking overpaid people's job title when we found one non-chief executive, which fulfilled the criterion for **Some**. There are other professions and individuals who fall under that description. Only some overpaid people are chief executives.

So, the predicate *hideously overpaid* is not distributed.

The final type is type **O**:

Some birthday presents are not Ferraris

Again, the word *some* tells us that not all members of the class of birthday presents are included in the premise. You could imagine checking all the birthday gifts, sifting through the ties and socks until we found at least one Ferrari in a bow (to make sure the situation isn't **All** or **No**).

So, the subject *some birthday presents* is not distributed.

Are Ferraris accounted for? Yes, because within the premise all Ferraris are some birthday presents and not some birthday presents. In this case, all Ferraris have been included. Accordingly, the predicate in this proposition is distributed.

Therefore, the predicate *Ferraris* is distributed.

Here's a summary showing where the subject or predicate of each type of argument is distributed:

Argument	Example	Distributed?
Type **A**: All … are	All golfers use golf clubs	Subject **is** distributed. Predicate **is not** distributed
Type **E**: No … are	No swimmer wears a suit of armour	Subject **is** distributed Predicate **is** distributed
Type **I**: Some … are	Some chief executives are hideously overpaid	Subject **is not** distributed Predicate **is not** distributed
Type **O**: Some … are not	Some birthday presents are not Ferraris	Subject **is not** distributed Predicate **is** distributed

That's it. All you need to know about distribution. It's only a little bit fiddly, but has a huge bearing on making syllogisms valid or not. Where were we?

Undistributed middle – part 2

Okay, back to where we were before our excursion, looking at our earlier example:

All thieves (middle term) are criminals (major term)

All embezzlers (minor term) are thieves (middle term)

Therefore, all embezzlers (minor term) are criminals (major term)

In this **A A A – 1** syllogism, the middle term *thieves* is distributed in the major premise. This means that the syllogism is valid. Fireworks! Streamers!

If we look at an example in which the middle term is not distributed, it suffers from the fallacy of the undistributed middle. This is in the form **A A A – 2** and it's not on the list of valid syllogisms.

All gorillas love sleeping

All students love sleeping

Therefore, all students are gorillas (invalid)

The middle term is love sleeping. It's in the **All A are B** type, but as the predicate in both premises, and as the subject in neither. Accordingly, the middle term is not distributed. Put another way, the middle term doesn't link gorillas and students, except for a shared love of sleeping. We can't infer any information from one about the other. The syllogism is therefore invalid, and the conclusion is a non sequitur, despite a certain resonance.

Rule: The middle term must be distributed in the premises at least once. If not, we have the fallacy of the undistributed middle.

Illicit major

The fallacy of the illicit major sounds like a yarn by Conan Doyle. In fact, it's a similar problem to the undistributed middle. It's a formal fallacy that renders an argument invalid.

The fault arises because the major term is not distributed in the major premise. (Now aren't you glad you know all about distribution?) Remember: the major term is the part of the major premise that appears as the predicate in the conclusion:

> All interns are unpaid labour
>
> No HR directors are interns
>
> Therefore, no HR directors are unpaid labour (invalid)

Ain't that the truth. It sounds valid enough, because the conclusion makes sense – we never see HR directors trying to get copier toner off business attire[4] and fretting about how to pay for their commute into work.

The major term *unpaid labour* is not distributed in the major premise (**All A are B**). The class of unpaid labour extends beyond interns, so it's not fully accounted for.

This example, therefore, suffers from the fallacy of an illicit major. It follows the form **A E E – 1**, which is not one of the valid syllogisms. In other words, no syllogism in this form can be valid.

> Rule: The major term must be distributed in the major premise. If it isn't, and is distributed in the conclusion instead, it's an illicit major.

Illicit minor

This sounds like a cheeky kid with fake ID trying to get served in a bar. It is, of course, the winsome sibling to the illicit major fallacy. It occurs when the minor term is not distributed in the minor premise. For instance:

---

[4] Cold water, not hot.

All trees have leaves

All trees have roots

Therefore, all roots have leaves (invalid)

The minor term *have roots* is not distributed in the minor premise. It leads to a conclusion that makes no sense. It follows the form **A A A – 3**, which is not one of the valid syllogisms.

Rule: The minor term must be distributed in the minor premise. If it isn't and is distributed in the conclusion instead, it's an illicit minor.

Exclusive premises

This logical fallacy sounds like a well-appointed pub. If only. Just as we can tie ourselves in knots when we make statements with multiple negatives, so do syllogisms. If we pack negative statements into both major and minor premises, the resulting mess is invalid. This is the fallacy of exclusive premises.

Here's the problem: in reasoning, propositions that are negative exclude one another. So if an argument has two negative premises, it means the middle term (which is supposed to link the two premises, allowing us to draw an inference about one term from the other) is locked out from both the major and minor premise. There's no connection between the two. As a result, it's not possible to reach a logical conclusion.

No cats are dogs

Some dogs are not poodles

Therefore, some poodles are not cats (invalid)

The middle term *dogs* appears correctly in both premises, and it's distributed in the major premise (in the

No A are B form). It should link them, but the two negative statements exclude each other. The conclusion, such as it is, is not informative about poodles or cats in any sensible way, because no poodles are cats. The example follows the form **E O O – 4**. Again, it's not one of the valid syllogisms.

Rule: A syllogism cannot have two negative premises (types E or O). If it does, it is invalid because of the fallacy of exclusive premises.

Affirmative conclusion – one negative premise

If you look through the list of valid syllogisms, whenever one of the premises is negative – that is, type **E** or **O**, the conclusion is also negative – **E** or **O** – always. An affirmative conclusion – **A** or **I** – following a single negative premise doesn't work. For instance:

No trucks are ships

Some ships are submarines

Therefore, some submarines are trucks (invalid)

Clearly, something's gone awry here. The format of the argument is **E I I – 4**, which is not a valid syllogism. In fact, no valid syllogism has a negative premise and an affirmative conclusion.

Rule: If a syllogism has one negative premise (type E or O), the conclusion must be negative. If a conclusion is negative, the syllogism must contain a negative premise.

Negative conclusion – two affirmative premises

This fallacy doesn't need much explanation in the light of the previous section; the title says it all. A valid syllogism cannot produce a negative conclusion if both premises are positive. For example:

All whales are aquatic creatures

All whales are mammals

Therefore, no mammals are aquatic creatures (invalid)

The conclusion is self-evidently wrong – plenty of mammals are aquatic, including whales. The format of this syllogism, **A A E – 3** is not one of the listed valid arguments. In fact, no valid argument has a negative conclusion (type **E** or **O**) when both premises are affirmative, either **A** or **I**.

Rule: If both premises are affirmative, the conclusion must also be affirmative.

A last look around before we go

Having examined the rules for syllogisms and seen why so many are invalid, let's go back to the beginning. We looked at two examples of invalid reasoning. Simple question – what's wrong with them? Which fallacy is in play?

All creatures that fly have wings

No ostriches can fly

Therefore, no ostriches have wings (invalid)

Some creatures with wings can fly

All ostriches are creatures with wings

Therefore, some ostriches can fly (invalid)

And here we leave syllogisms using quantifiers. Next is the family of deductive reasoning that uses propositions to reach a conclusion: *if... then* statements.

Hypothetical arguments

In this section, we don't need to concern ourselves with quantifiers like **All**, **No** and **Some**. Feel free to loosen your tie or kick off your shoes. This next family of deductive reasoning uses more natural language and arguments are much less grindingly precise. Errors made in this area of reasoning are also called *propositional* or *conditional* fallacies.

Many propositions are compound statements. Inside they contain logical operators that link the different parts. These are words like: **And**, **Or**, **Not**, **If**, **Only if.** We're going to concentrate on conditional **if... then** statements, for example:

> If I need to submit this report by Monday, then the intern's going to have a busy weekend.

These are the arguments you will come across most often. In everyday speech, the word *then* is omitted, but the reasoning remains the same. Here's what the reasoning in a hypothetical syllogism looks like:

> If P then Q,
>
> If Q then R
>
> Therefore, if P then R

This chain of possible consequences crops up a great deal in everyday life:

> If I fall off my roof, (then) I will injure myself
>
> If I injure myself, (then) I can't go hiking
>
> Therefore, if I fall off my roof, (then) I can't go hiking (valid)

A hypothetical syllogism is a valid inference. It's sometimes called a *chain argument* because of the way the premises string together.

For a compound proposition to be true, the components must satisfy the logical connectives. Hypothetical fallacies crop up when we infer something that the logical connectors can't guarantee to be correct.

In the format: If P, then Q, the P phrase is called an *antecedent* because it's the bit that comes first. The Q part is a *consequent* because if the antecedent is true, the consequent is the thing that ensues.

What we need is a statement which tells us that one of P or Q is true or false. If a premise agrees something is true, it *affirms*. If not true, it *denies*. Depending on the answer, we can then conclude something about P from Q being true or false, and we can infer something about Q if P is true or false.

Put together, they form a family of arguments which you will hear every single day of your life, as we try to figure out what the consequences of our choices will entail. Often the conclusions will be untrue.

It's important to pay close attention to the premises used in hypothetical arguments. On occasion, people use what sounds like deductive reasoning to add the semblance of rigour to what is really an opinion or assertion, rather than a true statement. In other words, some statements that sound like propositions are really bare assertions, which is a claim made without evidence. When that happens:

> "What can be asserted without evidence can be dismissed without evidence."[5]

---

[5] Christopher Hitchens, Slate Magazine, 2003.

Because who needs to be popular when you're right?

Affirming the consequent

Let's start with the hire-car dilemma:

If I put diesel into a petrol car, then the engine will be damaged [consequent]

The engine of my car is damaged [affirming]

Therefore, I have put diesel in the tank (invalid)

The argument is invalid because putting the wrong fuel in is not the only thing that can damage the engine. The form is:

If P, then Q

Q is true

Therefore, P is true (invalid)

This is the general form of an affirming the consequent argument. We can only reach a true conclusion if the antecedent is the only condition for the consequent we affirm. So both premises can be true, but the conclusion false, which means the argument must be invalid in all circumstances.

If a creature is human, then it has two legs

This creature has two legs

Therefore, this creature is human (invalid)

That would be a big promotion for my budgie. Affirming the consequent can be a fertile source of poor excuses. Take illness. The internet lets us diagnose any symptoms we imagine we have, and many people customise their reasoning to reach the conclusion they want:

If I have flu, then I have a headache

I do have a headache

Therefore, I have flu (invalid)

Flu isn't the only sufficient cause of headache – late-night partying might be another. You can picture someone starting with the conclusion that they want a day off, and working back to find an excuse.

Note that if the antecedent condition were in the form **if and only if,** then the conclusion would be valid. If having flu were the only condition to cause a headache, then affirming the headache would be proof of flu. But the *if and only if* condition is a stringent measure.

If and only if I score 21 with my first two cards do I get a blackjack.

An affirming the consequent argument only provides one logical certainty – a contrapositive. If the consequent is untrue, then the antecedent is also untrue. For example:

If I have arthritis, then I have a sore joint

My joint is sore

Therefore, I have arthritis (invalid)

My painful joint offers no certainty that I have arthritis. My injury could have been caused by a pole-dancing accident. But if I don't have a sore joint, I can conclude that I don't have arthritis. The contrapositive of affirming the consequent is denying the consequent.

This form of argument is a frequent visitor to conversations in which the speaker wants to force a conclusion with the semblance of logic. It's used as a means of sleight of hand, either deliberately, or when someone's just talking through their hat.

Denying the consequent

Denying the consequent is an important and logical argument. Labouring under the formal title *modus tollens*, this is a sort of anti-matter equivalent to affirming the consequent. Denying the consequent arguments are valid. Let's compare the two arguments:

Affirming the consequent:	Denying the consequent:
If P, then Q	If P, then Q
Q is true	Q is not true
Therefore, P is true (invalid)	Therefore, P is not true (valid)

Unlike affirming the consequent, denying the consequent allows us to make a valid inference about the antecedent. If the first two statements are true, the conclusion cannot be false. For instance:

If it's Thursday today, then it's bin day [consequent]

It's not bin day [denying]

Therefore, it's not Thursday today (valid)

Here, the absence of bin-related activity allows us to infer that it's not that particular day of the week. Another example of denying the consequent providing a valid inference:

If I hold a UK driving licence, then I am 17 years or older

I am not 17 years or older

Therefore, I do not hold a UK driving licence (valid)

Based on the structure of the argument, you can seemingly nix any consequent, and thereby invalidate the antecedent. It's a handy format to keep in mind if you have a point to prove.

"If that's justice, then I'm a banana," was the reaction of Ian Hislop, editor of Private Eye magazine, after losing a libel action. The editor is self-evidently not a yellow fruit,[6] and thus invited the world's press to conclude that the verdict was unjust.

Denying the consequent is an important form of reasoning:

> If Moriarty is the thief, then fingerprints on the Fabergé egg are his
>
> The fingerprints are not his
>
> Therefore, Moriarty is not the thief (valid)

It's the argument that excludes possibilities, exonerates, and rebuts wild theories:

> If the politician is the father, then a DNA test proves it
>
> The DNA test does not prove it
>
> Therefore, the politician is not the father (valid)

Denying the consequent is a valid argument provided the premises are sound. Sometimes people use sleight of hand to slide a bare assertion or a false promise into the mix. While the reasoning may be valid, the argument is unsound if the premise is doubtful. How about this conversation?

> "If you have nothing to hide, then you have nothing to be afraid of"
>
> "But I am afraid"
>
> "Therefore, you must have something to hide" (unsound)

Beware claims presented as truths: they can be a convincing sham:

---

[6] Technically, a banana is a herb. Strange, but true.

If our sales force works hard, then we can increase our revenues

We did not increase our revenues

Therefore, our sales force did not work hard (unsound)

In fact, there are many reasons why businesses don't grow sales. Lack of effort is one of them, but not the only one. And high levels of productivity isn't guaranteed to lead to success, either. Be alert to glib assertions disguised as an **if... then** premise.

Denying the antecedent

This cheerful title means no more than saying the hypothetical thing you just mentioned didn't happen or isn't true. It's a formal fallacy, and arguments in this form are invalid. The form is this:

If P, then Q

P is not true

Therefore, Q is not true (invalid)

Again, the antecedent is the *if* part of the opening premise. The denying part is the second premise telling us the antecedent isn't true:

If Towser is a St Bernard [antecedent], then he is a dog

Towser is not a St Bernard [denying]

Therefore, Towser is not a dog (invalid)

It's a conclusion that might come as a surprise to Mrs Towser, who is expecting his puppies and a bit of help around the kennel. Towser can be any one (or combination) of hundreds of breeds of hound besides a St Bernard. Here's another, oft-quoted example:

If it is raining, then the grass is wet

It is not raining

Therefore, the grass is not wet (invalid)

This argument overlooks the moisturising power of a sprinkler system. Or dew fall. Or Towser's continuing incontinence. At first sight, these kinds of argument can appear valid, especially with abstract ideas. But even where the premises ring true, the conclusion may not necessarily be true as well, which makes it an invalid form of argument.

Affirming the antecedent

The final part of our conditional family deals with affirming the antecedent. It suffers from the Latin moniker *modus ponens*, and it's an extremely common argument that stretches back into philosophical antiquity.

When the second premise affirms that the antecedent is true, the argument concludes that the consequent must be true. Which is what we began with in the first place – a kind of self-fulfilling prophecy. Unlike the previous form, denying the antecedent, this reasoning produces a valid argument.

Denying the antecedent	Affirming the antecedent
If P, then Q	If P, then Q
P is not true	P is true
Therefore, Q is not true (invalid)	Therefore, Q is true (valid)

For example:

If today is Monday [antecedent], I must go to work

Today is Monday [affirming]

Therefore, I must go to work (valid)

If the opening premises are true, that is, I have a regular job and today is a normal work day, then the conclusion has to be valid. That being the case, we can say the argument is a valid in form. But the validity of the argument doesn't mean the premises are true. If the premises are unsound, it nullifies any attempt at reasoning:

If it is the chairman's birthday, then aliens from Planet Zob must land

It is the chairman's birthday

Therefore, aliens...etc. (unsound)

The argument makes no comment on the quality, fairness or morality of the statements, only the reasoning used about them. If you want to give a logical veneer to any personal decision, this is the argument to go for. There's more than a whiff of a false dichotomy about many uses of this argument.

If my son's trainers are smelly, then they need to be left outdoors

My son's trainers are smelly

Therefore, they need to be left outdoors (valid)

Affirming the antecedent is a type of argument we encounter day to day – in the disguise of natural language:

If you want fairness for all and prosperity for your family, [then] you should vote for me

After all, isn't that what we all want? [affirming]

[Therefore, you should] Vote for me!

Okay, it's scarcely Churchillian, but you get the point. Affirming the antecedent allows you to present a seemingly logical conclusion to pretty much any statement. So, thinking of statements that lack a certain objective quality:

hello, advertising! Promotional statements are often based on shaky claims at best. The opening premise is often an assertion by the advertiser. Affirming the antecedent arguments (sort of) prove every claim. For instance:

> If I wear New Wolf-Sweat Fragrance for Men, then I will be attractive to women
>
> I am wearing New Wolf-Sweat Fragrance for Men
>
> Therefore, I am attractive to women

The argument is risible, but that's the mesmerical world of advertising for you. The other big use of this form of reasoning is to underpin the fallacy of necessity, the favourite tool of would-be decisive management. The fallacy of necessity is a formal error in which the inevitability of an outcome of events is applied to the action taken as a result.

> If we need to cut costs, then we must reduce our headcount
>
> We need to cut costs
>
> Therefore, we must reduce our headcount (unsound)

An affirming the antecedent form of argument seemingly confirms with unerring logic the action you wanted to take in the first place. It applies a varnish of rigour to a business choice. But it's a smokescreen. The opening premise may not be a true statement: the consequent is not the sole or necessary outcome to the antecedent, just a preferred course of action. Be warned.

Necessary conditions

In logic, necessity and sufficiency describe the type of conditional relationship between statements. A necessary condition looks like this:

> If P then Q

For example:

If it is raining, then it is cloudy

In this statement, P cannot be true unless Q is true. P implies Q. Accordingly, we can say that *Q is a necessary condition for P*. Rain needs cloud; no cloud, no rain. A pre-qualification requirement is a necessary condition:

If a UK law has been passed, then it has received Royal Assent

If I visit an island, then I must cross water on the way

If Mrs Hudson makes an omelette, then she must break some eggs

In claiming that *Q is necessary for P*, we're saying in formal terms that *P can't be true unless Q is true*, and that *if Q is false, then P is false* also. This means that *whenever P is true, so is Q*.

Necessary conditions where *if P then Q*	
P is true, then	Q is true
Q is true, then	P is true
P is false, then	Q is false
Q is false, then	P is false

Note that we're talking about a logically necessary condition, an inference, as distinct from a necessary cause:

If the cat knocks an ornament off the mantelpiece, then it smashes in the hearth

In necessary causes, the reasoning flows from the *if* clause to the *then* predicate. In logic, the necessary inference flows from the *then* clause back to the *if*:

If the ornament is smashed in the hearth, then the cat has knocked it off the mantelpiece

Sufficient conditions

In sufficient conditions where *If P then Q,* knowing that P is true means we have enough information to conclude that Q is also true.

If the monarch is a king, then the monarch is male

If Alice is top of the class, then she has the best overall marks

If a novel is out of copyright, then its author has been dead for over 70 years[7]

In each example, we have sufficient information in *P* to conclude that *Q* must be true. This can be expressed as *P is true only if Q is true* and as *P implies Q*. However, if P is false, we don't have sufficient information to infer that Q is false. For instance:

If Jordan is an actress, then Jordan is a woman (sufficient)

If Jordan is not an actress, then Jordan is not a woman (not sufficient)

If Jordan is not an actress, then he or she may be in any occupation and be of either sex. If the P component is false, we simply have no valid inference to draw upon. We have something akin to an ox-bow lake of reasoning.

We can construct a grid of the possible outcomes of sufficient conditions, depending on whether P and Q are true or false. It becomes obvious there are three possible outcomes:

---

[7] Under EU law. The situation under US law is different.

Sufficient conditions where *if P then Q*	
P is true, then	Q is true
Q is true, then	P is true
P is false, then	No valid inference about Q
Q is false, then	P is false

Conditions both necessary and sufficient

Conditions can be either necessary, sufficient or both. For instance:

If today is Christmas Day, then it is 25th December

If today is Thursday, then yesterday was Wednesday

If today is Thursday, we have sufficient information to know that yesterday was Wednesday, and that yesterday must necessarily have been Wednesday. Yesterday being Wednesday is both a sufficient and necessary condition for today being Thursday.

Where a condition is both necessary and sufficient, it's the equivalent of saying:

P if and only if Q, and Q if and only if P

P is necessary and sufficient for Q, and Q is necessary and sufficient for P

Each of these statements applies to the examples above:

Today is Christmas Day if and only if it is 25th December

It is 25th December if and only if it is Christmas Day

Being Thursday today is necessary and sufficient to know yesterday was Wednesday

Yesterday being Wednesday is necessary and sufficient to know today is Thursday

If and only if is a bi-conditional statement in which the connected statements, P and Q, are both true or both false. (This is expressed as **iff** in some fields.) It's distinct from the component conditions *if* and *only if*. For instance:

If it is a Fabergé egg, then Moriarty will steal the object

Here we learn Moriarty will steal jewels that are Fabergé eggs. He might also steal tiaras, necklaces and other jewels. That the jewellery is a Fabergé egg is a **sufficient** condition for Moriarty to take it. He will steal every Fabergé egg he happens upon.

Only if it is a Fabergé egg will Moriarty steal the object

Moriarty is choosy enough to steal only Fabergé eggs. But he won't necessarily steal it if an opportunity presents itself. Here, being a Fabergé egg is a **necessary** condition for Moriarty to purloin it, but it is not a sufficient condition, since he might not take it.

If and only if it is a Fabergé egg will Moriarty steal the object

In this version, Moriarty will steal every Fabergé egg he can lay his hands on, but no other objet d'art. It is both a **necessary and sufficient** condition that the piece be a Fabergé egg for Moriarty to steal it.

In conclusion, it's clear that larceny may be illegal, but it is logical.

The fallacy of necessity

The fallacy of necessity is a formal error that managers often fall for. It's an argument that takes the inevitability of some outcome of a premise and transfers it to the consequent.

> If Mrs Hudson is a widow, then her husband has died. She is a widow, therefore Mr Hudson had to die

Becoming a widow is an automatic consequence of her husband dying; no-one had to be killed. Put technically, the fallacy comes about when we muddle:

- the inevitability of a consequence with
- the necessity of the consequent

For example:

> If someone falls from a high place they will inevitably be injured or killed, therefore high places must be protected by railings

This fallacy arises often when someone gets a bee in their bonnet about a particular course of action, and justifies it by attaching it to an unavoidable cause and effect:

> Motorcyclists are 20 times more like to be killed than car drivers, therefore motorcycles must be banned. (invalid)[8]

The reason motorcycles are less safe in an accident than cars is self-evident. It is inevitable that the fatality rate must be higher than with cars. It is not, however, a necessity to equalise the two fatality rates, nor is banning motorcycles the only way to improve matters. If the overriding necessity were to achieve safe forms of transport, cars would be banned in favour of aircraft.

---

[8] In 2016, Warren Truss, Australia's Federal Minister for Infrastructure and Regional Development, told parliament that motorcyclists were 20 times more likely to be killed than car users, so motorcycles must be phased out on Australia's roads. Cue laughter on a global scale.

The conclusions of many discussions and meetings in business end with a statement of necessity, something like:

In the current poor trading climate, our profits will inevitably fall...

Therefore, we must raise our prices by X per cent

Therefore, we have to cut our human assets by Y

Therefore, we have no choice but to squeeze suppliers, etc

In the vast majority of cases, these 'necessary' conclusions are bogus. None is inevitable. The decision is often couched in a formula of words like this:

I see no other choice...

Better to act decisively...

It is with great reluctance that I conclude...

I don't like this any more than you...

These glib emollients translate as:

We're choosing a course of action that's a) best for the people who run the business, and b) best for the people who own it. If you were more important, you'd be in one of those two groups.

In many descriptions of the fallacy of necessity, we can find a version of this:

Sherlock is a bachelor. A bachelor is unmarried. Therefore, Sherlock cannot get married. (invalid)

As we ponder the flawed reasoning, we know that whatever conditions, labels, or circumstances have brought him to that point, Sherlock can do anything he chooses. The same applies to business managers. There are very few necessary course of action, apart from those involving the tax authorities.

Either … or …

A disjunctive syllogism is a proposition unlike the others. It doesn't start with a condition, but with what looks like a choice. A disjunctive syllogism is a valid rule of inference. It runs like this:

Either P or Q is true

P is not true

Therefore, Q is true

Affirming or denying a disjunct

This argument gives us two apparent alternatives (called *disjuncts*) linked by an *or* statement. We learn that one of options is true (or false). We infer the remaining option is false (or true). For instance:

The teacher will mark homework or open a bottle of wine [two disjuncts]

The teacher will open a bottle of wine [affirming]

Therefore, the teacher will not mark homework (valid)

The conclusion is valid. The opening statement offers us two disjuncts. The second premise affirms one of them is true. We conclude that the remaining disjunct is false. This argument is called *affirming a disjunct*. Alternatively, the second premise can refute one of the disjuncts – *denying a disjunct* – and so we can conclude the remaining option must be true.

So far, so good. Now the big *however*. Up to now, we've been presuming that the disjuncts are exclusive. An **exclusive-or** means **either / or**. Only one statement is true, but not both:

The plant on my terrace is a clematis or a rose

The plant is not a rose   [denying]

Therefore, the plant is a clematis   (valid)

Here, only one disjunct can be true. The plant can't be both a clematis and a rose. If the premise is true – the plant is not a rose – then it must be a clematis. In everyday language, we most often intend an exclusive-or:

Let's go and see the new film on Friday or Saturday

This afternoon I plan to go shopping or dig the garden

The teacher decided to open a bottle of wine. Red or white, she mused

Exclusive-or arguments look like this:

P is true [exclusive-] or Q is true	P is true [exclusive-] or Q is true
Q is true [affirming]	Q is false [denying]
Therefore, P is false (valid)	Therefore, P is true (valid)

In technical contexts, the exclusive-or version is sometimes expressed as EOR or XOR to signify an operation that returns the value *true* when either of the disjuncts is true and the other is false, but not when both are not-true and both are not-false.

Inclusive-or

While in everyday English, *or* usually means exclusive-or, in formal reasoning (say, mathematics, logic, programming, etc.) *or*, the logical conjunction, is inclusive. Inclusive–or means *and / or*. This means that either or both statements can be true:

My neighbour's noisy dog is aggressive or badly trained

The dog is badly trained

Therefore, the dog is not aggressive (invalid)

Obviously, my neighbour's noisy animal can be both aggressive and badly trained. In inclusive logical expressions, both disjuncts can be true or just one of them. This means that affirming an inclusive-or disjunct can lead to an invalid inference that the other disjunct must be false.

Conversely, when an argument denies a disjunct, it is a valid inference that the other is true, and this is the case with both exclusive-or and inclusive-or constructions.

P is true [inclusive-] or Q is true	P is true [inclusive-] or Q is true
Q is true [affirming]	Q is false [denying]
Therefore, P is false (invalid)	Therefore, P is true (valid)

To conclude: we need to be sure whether the statement we're interpreting is informal language or intended to be a more formal deduction. Generally, if the statement we're questioning is intended to be exclusive, the presence of either / or is a good start. The context should confirm our interpretation:

This drink is either beer or wine

Unless we're quaffing the worst cocktail in the world, that statement is pretty unambiguous. If we intend to convey an inclusive meaning, it might be appropriate (even if inelegant) to make that clear using *and / or*:

Let's go to the cinema on Friday and / or go for a meal on Saturday

A word of warning: if you're presented with a hard-and-fast choice between P or Q, be wary of being offered a false dichotomy. Getting a 'mark' to focus on two red herrings is how clever sleight-of-hand artists slide an idea past us.

JOINED-UP CONNECTIONS

For completeness, it's worth making sure we cover the other common logical connectives. If you're interested in maths or programming, you'll know these and more by heart. But for the rest of us, a reminder won't go amiss. The topic of logical operations is a huge and steep one. It demands a clear mind and a decent run-up to clear the summit. So this list is just a hint of the main meanings you might have to clamber over most often.

A new word: *operands*. These are the statements controlled by the connective words. The disjuncts mentioned earlier in this section are operands. In reasoning, we try to find a valid argument, while logic identifies statements that are true or false. The way connectives work, however, is much the same:

And – a conjunction – valid / true if both (or all) operands are true:

> To be an effective cruise liner, a ship must have accommodation for passengers and be able to float.

Or (inclusive) – true if one or both operands is true:

> For my birthday, I'd be happy to get a book or a DVD.

Neither... nor – the negation of logical *or*. When neither operand is true (both are false):

> Because Moriarty was in Switzerland at the time, police can neither arrest him nor charge him with robbing the mansion in Penge.

Either... or (exclusive) – true only when operands differ; one is true and the other is false:

> The two dogs were alone in the house while we were out. Either Towser left us a present on the rug or Mrs Towser

did. The goldfish is in the clear for purely logistical reasons.

If... then – the consequent is true if the antecedent is true:

> If my car passes its annual inspection then I can drive it legally.

Only if – introducing a material condition that means for the antecedent to be true, the consequent must also be true:

> The astronaut knew she would survive only if her oxygen supply lasted until help arrived.

If and only if – either both operands are true, or both are false:

> If and only if this is the right password, then we can hack into the company's bank account.

Not both / not and – at least one operand is false:

> Perhaps our intern really does have a pet called Joey, but it can not be both a budgie and a kangaroo

Now we're done with syllogisms in all their subtle brevity. It's time to address other formal fallacies. These are arguments that defy a rule of logic and are invalid.

OTHER FORMAL FALLACIES

Leaving syllogisms behind, there are a small number of formal fallacies that all private deductives need to be aware of. On the surface, the case being made might sound as wholesome and filling as grandma's fruit cake. Beware the get-out-of-jail file baked inside these logical jaw-breakers.

Bad reasons fallacy

Also known as the *fallacy fallacy*, this formal howler comes about when we realise that the reason or thinking behind a certain conclusion is bad, so we decide that the conclusion is false, invalid or incorrect. But even a broken clock is right twice a day. It's a fallacy almost custom-made for someone who understands a little about reasoning, but not enough. For instance:

> CEOs need a chauffeur because they can't parallel park a car

It may be true that Les Grands Fromages of this world need a driver, but it almost certainly isn't because they lack parking skills, at least in general. We can't rule out the clamour for chauffeurs simply because the argument used is weak, if not absolutely wrong.

If you've ever heard yourself say that someone is right for the wrong reasons, you've already encountered this teaser.

Appeal to probability

Appeal to probability is the error of assuming that something definitely will happen because it might possibly happen. It means taking something for granted because it would probably be the case.

"Sod's law. If it can go wrong, it will do."

"We don't need any contingency plan. It'll probably never happen."

"I bet those snipers couldn't hit a barn door from…"

Its sister is called *appeal to possibility*, a spurious argument carrying a strong whiff of blind optimism in some remotely possible occurrence.

"Now, cheer up. You're going to be with us for a long time. There are researchers all over the world looking for a cure."

"His execution might not happen. The president can grant a reprieve at any point before the deadline. Oh, did I just say *dead*?"

"I've chosen the yacht I'm going to buy. I just need this lottery ticket to win us the money. What shall we call it?"

As with all fallacies, the conclusion isn't supported by the facts. In this case, you can't reach a firm conclusion solely because an event is technically possible, or at least not impossible. The error is to assume an outcome has a probability of 0 or 1, when in fact it lies anywhere in between.

Base rate fallacy

Base rate refers to general or background information. It's often the big picture data that sets the stage for an event of inference. So, when presented with specific information that pertains in one instance, we tend to focus on that and ignore the background data. It's a formal fallacy.

Here's a simple example:

You see a pale-skinned, red-haired man hiding from the sun under a beach umbrella,. He's reading an English-language newspaper. Is he more likely to be Scottish or

American? Isn't that a simple fifty-fifty, yes or no sort of situation?

We think of red hair as a Celtic colouration, reinforced by the many stereotypes of Scottishness from the historically risible film *Braveheart* to Groundskeeper Willie in *The Simpsons*. If you know your gingers too, you'll plump for Scottish. Scotland has the highest incidence of red hair in the world, around 13 per cent of the population – some 690,000 people.

Among Americans, the incidence is only somewhere between two and five per cent. But the population of the USA is about 316 million. That means there are at least 6.3 million gingers with American accents, perhaps several millions more, and certainly more than the entire population of Scotland.

All things being equal, our pale pal is ten times – an order of magnitude – more likely to be American than Scottish. Plumping for Scotland might have seemed the better bet. But the relevant base rate (the prior probability) here is the population size of the USA compared to Scotland's. In fact, despite the small percentage, its large population means the USA has the biggest number of red-haired citizens in the world.

Moving on, many business managers conflate two immensely important factors in performance (of people, products, and so on): false positive and false negative indications. They aren't the same thing.

Suppose a country has a population of 50 million. Assume there are 1,000 terrorists actively plotting murder and mayhem.

The likelihood of a good citizen randomly stopped being a terrorist killer is 1,000 in 50 million, that is 0.002 per cent.

Correspondingly, the chance that the person stopped is not a terrorist is 99.998 per cent. Agreed?

> To help find the killers, the government introduces surveillance cameras with face-recognition software. The supplier assures the government the system has a false positive and a false negative both of one per cent.

This means that if the system spots a killer, it raises an alarm 99 per cent of the time, but fails to alert security folks one per cent of the time (a false negative). However, when the system sifts through ordinary tax-payers and voters, no alarm will be raised 99 per cent of the time, but on one per cent of occasions an alert will be raised (a false positive).

> One day, your sweet, kindly mother triggers an alarm. The security operative confuses the one per cent false positive (which this is) with the one per cent false negative (where ninety-nine killers in a hundred get caught). The operative infers there's a 99 per cent chance that your mother is a killer. Clang! resounds the jail door.

The number of alarms per innocent citizen (false positive) and the number of killers per non-alarm (false negative) are a long way apart, because the two groups are hugely different in size (like the populations of Scotland and the USA).

> Suppose that, sooner or later, the identity system scans the whole population of 50 million people. Some 990 of the 1,000 killers trigger the alarm. Ten killers are left at large to carry on committing mayhem – that's the one per cent false negative at play.
>
> Among the 49,999,000 citizens scanned by the system, however, 499,990 also set off the alarm – a one per cent false positive. In a total of 500,980 alarms, therefore, just 990 will actually be killers.
>
> So when the alarm goes off, the odds that a person

triggering it actually is a killer, therefore, is 990 ÷ 500,980, a smidge under 0.2 per cent. That's a vanishingly small hit rate, and a long way shy of the supposedly intuitive figure of 99 per cent.

In a nutshell, this fallacy conflates false negative (killers on the loose) and false positive (citizens wrongly accused). When security people think that an alarm means there's a 99 per cent chance we're a terrorist, it goes a long way to explain their disgraceful treatment of innocent travellers at airports in supposedly free countries.

Now imagine you work for an employer who arrogates the moral right to control what employees do in the 128 hours per week they're not at work or being paid. Testing employees for drugs is a fun way to impose our self-righteous ethical codes on others.

Usually, tests are standard kits administered and processed en masse by operatives of, let's say, average capability. Drugs tests routinely produce false positives at a rate between five and ten per cent (and occasionally much higher) depending on the quality of the lab analysing the tests. That's the true base rate here. Meanwhile, labs claim false positives and false negatives of under one per cent. Well, they would.

> After, say, 1,000 employees are tested, you appear among the 50 to 100 completely clean colleagues who show up as false positives (five to 10 per cent). Your employer wrongly infers that since false positives are claimed to be under one per cent, it's therefore 99 per cent likely that you've been having fun of a kind it doesn't endorse.

> Even so, the employer allows you all to re-take the test, just to make sure your lawyers are happy. Among the 50 to 100 retakes, you end up in the group of 3 to 10 people who yet again show up as a false positive. What are the odds, then, that you're entirely innocent?

Well, the employer is mesmerised by the claimed false positive of one per cent, and believes it's one in 99 multiplied by one in 99. That is, the mighty brains think the odds of you innocently failing two drug tests is one in 9,801, or 0.01 per cent.

Put another way, you're fired, Lebowski, and some folks in the Human Capital team get paid a bonus for weeding out yet another lying junkie.

The thing that killed your career is a trust in the claimed false-positive rate of less than one per cent. That's a dream number, a figure the laboratory sales people used to sell their services to the employer. The real base rate, the prior probability, is a false positive of five to ten per cent.

If the lab or the employer looked at the second test results, and realised that 90 to 95 per cent of the supposedly positive results from the first test came back clean, the company should see that the false-positive rate is running at five to ten per cent. That's high enough to leave between three (actually, 2.5) and ten innocent employees failing two tests.

And just in case any employer still thinks it's a good idea to test employees en masse, false negative rates are routinely between ten and 15 per cent. Of the 1,000 people tested in our example, up to 100 or 150 could be slavering dope fiends and still get a completely clean bill of health. Still think it's money well spent?

The base rate fallacy tells us we ignore the bigger picture, wider context and background information at our peril.

Proof by example

Inappropriate generalisation is another name for this logical fallacy. It crops up when we claim one or more examples offer proof for a general principal. While generalisation stokes the furnace of inference, proof by example hints at a deductively certain extrapolation. For instance:

> One member of parliament charged personal costs to parliamentary expenses, therefore all MPs are fraudulent.

> Our head of purchasing lives in a luxury penthouse apartment, so all purchasing specialists live above their means.

> We don't recruit graduates from Cambridge University because we once hired someone who didn't work out in our organisation.

Proof by example is a favourite tactic of management consultants selling their wares. They point to a successful organisation that supposedly works in a way that the management phrenologists recommend to other organisations. The living proof anoints the firm's advice with some sort of holy chrism, making it applicable to a universal commercial audience, regardless of all the many factors that influence an organisation's success.

A proof by example is only valid as a singular premise to an existential conclusion. That means, a situation where a single instance proves that situation or event is at all possible:

> Somebody swam the Channel, therefore it is possible to swim the Channel.

> The *Miracle on the Hudson* proved a jet airliner could land intact on water.

> Edmund Hillary and Tenzing Norgay climbed Mount Everest. Therefore it is possible to climb the world's tallest mountain.

Other than these kinds of instances, single examples offer no reason to infer the event is more than a one-off outlier.

Conjunction fallacy

A conjunction is just two things linked together. If each item is true separately, they are true together.

If P is true and Q is true

Then, P + Q is true

Deductively, this is a valid argument because both conjuncts are individually stated to be true. The conjunction fallacy crops up when we assume that some specific conditions linked together are more likely than a single, broader outcome. In general, it operates like this:

Which do you believe? Statement A, or statement A plus B?

I'll take A plus B, please.

It's a bit like betting on a football team, and getting odds of 10/1 against winning the match, but odds of only 2/1 against winning by more than five goals. Winning by a big margin is a subset of mere winning, and much less likely than a victory with any winning score. The conjunction of a) a win and b) a big goal difference must be less probable than a simple win. A conjunct can never be more probable than the chances of any component part alone.

How is it possible we believe a convoluted set of circumstances is more likely than a simple explanation? Well, psychologists observe that people just do. As the young say: *it's a thing*. Plus there's the good, old-fashioned conspiracy theory:

I don't believe in coincidences. There's something behind

all this. No smoke without fire.

It's a odd quirk of human thinking that we imagine a complicated arrangement to be more likely than a simpler situation on its own. We're good at putting two and two together and making a hash of it.

We can't apply a deductive conclusion to random connections and assume a pattern of intentional events.

Masked man fallacy

This fallacy is a bit of a logical stinker, even though it crops up every day in the office and elsewhere. It's also called the *illicit substitution of identicals*, which hints at a certain complexity. It's a fallacy so formal it wears a morning suit and top hat in the shower.

First, the title comes from this kind of scenario:

I know who Moriarty is

I don't know who the masked man is

Therefore, Moriarty is not the masked man (invalid)

That's clearly an invalid argument, since Moriarty is perfectly capable of running a double life. The premises may be true, but the conclusion invalid. It's possible the person I know and the mysterious stranger are one and the same.

Suppose the two people (or things or expressions) really are the same, and we can have two categorical premises:

Elton John recorded *Candle in the Wind*

Reginald Dwight is Elton John's real name

Therefore, Reginald Dwight recorded *Candle in the Wind* (valid)

Swapping the terms Elton John and Reginald Dwight is valid because they are the same person. The second premise tells us categorically that this is the case. So the conclusion contains no more information than we've been given. There are no extra inferences or assumptions. Swapping the names is a valid substitution of identicals. But suppose the premise was:

> John Peel said that Elton John recorded *Candle in the Wind*.

We couldn't then conclude:

> John Peel said that Reginald Dwight recorded *Candle in the Wind*. (invalid)

That's not what he said. In putting those words in John Peel's mouth, we've made an illicit substitution of identicals. We reached a conclusion by inferring more information than the premise supplied, namely that Elton and Reginald are one and the same. It doesn't matter if the conclusion turns out to be true; the argument is deductively invalid.

Note also that the information is reported speech ("John Peel said that..."). It's an example of *intensional context* which warns us the information is not a categorical fact, just someone's attitude towards the information. Examples of intensional contexts include:

- Propositional attitudes: When we...

> Say that / know that / fear that / hope that / believe that / report that / desire that / suspect that / understand that / write that, and so on

...we're proposing information that's less than unassailably certain. Only categorical premises offer valid, deductive conclusions.

- Modal contexts, which happen when we say that something...

Can / may / must / could / should / would, etc occur

... or that it is...

... forbidden, obligatory, permitted, or will necessarily, probably, possibly, etc be the case

Here, again, we're asserting information that's less than categorical. Again, premises that are less than categorical cannot produce a deductively valid conclusion.

When we swap supposed identicals within intensional contexts we reach an invalid conclusion. For instance:

Mrs Hudson believed the street urchin was drunk. The boy was Wiggins. Therefore Wiggins was drunk. (invalid)

The blackmailer was probably left-handed. Milverton is not left-handed. Therefore, the blackmailer is not Milverton. (invalid)

The burglar possibly had a moustache. Lestrade has a moustache. Therefore, Lestrade was the burglar. (invalid)

It's clear that anyone who has to investigate crime, accidents or other events, and evaluate evidence from witnesses, must navigate through intensional contexts which make statements much less reliable. In conversation, we summarise the events we're talking about. We slide in and out of propositional and modal phraseology without thinking. We allow listeners to wrongly infer that we've made a factual statement.

At work, we have to carefully pick our way through fact, opinion, rumour, belief, and so on, in order to make decisions about what is really happening.

Let's examine just one aspect of working life – meetings. These give rise to the greatest works of fiction in any language – minutes. Minutes are summaries of discussions, decisions and action points. They are (supposedly)

contemporaneous notes that are subsequently approved as accurate by the people who attended the meeting.

Suppose the minutes say:

> Marketing reports the new product range could be delayed by a month at least.

Everyone eligible for a bonus is suddenly awake. Calls are made. The marketing head is invited to have a chat with the CEO. The financial director has already pointed out the cash-flow implications, because accountants are good at bad news and fear. The HR director has dusted down the personal goals for every member of the marketing team to be certain how far up the organisation this catastrophe can be blamed.

What actually happened? One of the marketing product managers, Nadia, was at a meeting:

> Chair: "What's happening with the new product range?"
>
> Nadia: "Everything's on track, apart from a yellow flag on electrical safety testing. The lab has said there might possibly be a delay over the long public holiday weekend."
>
> Chair: "What's the worst case?"
>
> Nadia: "If we have a delay of a few days, nothing changes. But if it's more than a week, we could miss the scheduled design sign-off, which might delay our production confirmation to the factory in China. They might miss the main sea-container shipping deadline, so we'd probably have to air-freight the launch stock to Europe."
>
> Chair: "That's going to be more expensive. How much later would the launch stock arrive if we shipped it all the way by sea?"
>
> Nadia: "Over a month."
>
> Chair: "Okay, so that's the worst, worst case."

Nadia: "We'll keep an eye on it…"

The minutes were confusingly terse. Nadia was riffing on a *what-if* conjecture. Moreover, most of Nadia's speculation was embedded in the modal context: *possibly, if, could, might, probably*. The minutes even begin with a propositional attitude ("reports") which should be a flag to readers, but all the other intensional contexts from Nadia at the meeting have been washed away, turning what was, at worst, an advisory footnote into a categorical cash-flow disaster.

A huge amount of unnecessary management conflict arises from misreporting and misinterpreting information arising from the masked man fallacy. We infer information that may not be factually accurate; we substitute categorical statements for remarks couched in uncertainty; we offer strawman arguments as a substitute for what someone actually said.

We need to double-check who precisely did or said what. Get the actual words used. Pay attention to modal phrasing. We could, of course, actually ask the person involved:

"Nadia, I may have the wrong end of the stick, but is there going to be any delay launching the new range?"

"No, it's all on track. Why do you ask?"

"Nothing. My mistake."

The moral is to make intensional contexts clear, and to give them only the weight they're due. To do that, listen to what people actually say, rather than what you imagine they're telling you. Ask them to clarify what they're saying. Be scrupulously careful about passing on second-hand, hearsay information. Don't add any more meaning or information that you or others have inferred. If you don't know the facts, say so. Most importantly, don't jump to conclusions. Your native confirmation bias will lead you directly to the result you prefer, want, expect or are afraid to see, not what is actually happening.

The ability to evaluate information accurately is an essential business quality. Organisations are a soup of data, information, rumour, speculation, assumption, conjecture, gossip and opinion. Here's a phrase you could usefully deploy:

> "Please tell me only the facts you know for certain. When I need some guesswork, I'll be sure to ask for it."

Any information we get or give that isn't solid fact is a mere guess. An opinion is not even a guess. Anyone can have an opinion on any topic under the sun – actual, hypothetical, surreal or whimsical – but it can never amount to a logical conclusion.

Having delved deep into the mechanics of argument, it's useful to know when and how to apply our powers of deduction.

Remember, the purpose of deductive reasoning is to reach valid conclusions. By contrast, abductive reasoning examines possible hypotheses to find likely causes. Inductive reasoning infers connections between outcomes and causes, and inference is susceptible to all manner of faulty thinking.

Everyday life is a mixture of informal chat, gossip, misinformation and bare assertion. We see and hear entire debates in the media – moderated arguments – based on supposition and opinion-as-fact. The overwhelming majority of premises used in these arguments are hopelessly unsound. In the office, far too much management time is wasted chasing the ghosts of truth and the smoke of rumour. Remember Nadia's marketing report and the misapprehension of intensional contexts?

Confirm the premises of any argument

The premise to every argument is an open invitation to sleight of hand. An individual just has to slide their 'facts' in, let reasoning fill its sails, and watch the argument cruise to the destination they want. So if you're trying to navigate an argument or discern a truth, be sceptical about every premise presented to you. It may concern a specific action, wider policy, business direction, choice of supplier, customer offering, anything. It's not cynicism; it's your job.

Any information that is not directly supported by empirical evidence is likely to be a belief or an opinion, Sometimes the only supporting evidence is a claim that the information is common knowledge ("everybody knows...") – that's a fallacious argument. If a premise is widely accepted, that merely proves the belief is popular, not that it's true. Get confirmation from objective, independent sources.

Unless all parties to a discussion agree the premises of an argument are true and sound, the information needs to be double-checked. Don't let colleagues get away with a bare assertion. In this context, *colleague* includes *boss*. Unless you know the statement they're relying on is true, challenge or investigate it. Don't casually accept it. Being agreeable is no substitute for effective management.

Wrinkles in the cloth of reasoning

Because life isn't simple, and because problems can be subtle, we must illuminate investigations with some important axioms of reasoning.

Above all else, the burden of proof lies with the party making a claim or assertion. If your marketing guru tells you customers don't like model X, flavour Y, or colour Z, they need to show you evidence. It's not your responsibility to prove them wrong. Any claim presented without argument can be dismissed without argument. The best argument is evidence.

Sometimes, something as mundane as a motto or axiom is repeated so often it adopts a truth-like form in an organisation's mind. Corporate slogans are a case in point. These especially must by examined if decisions are going to be based on them, otherwise they're just wishful thinking on a corporate level, just dollar-driven dreams.

That said, some true things may never be proven categorically true; some false things may never be conclusively disproved. That's just the way it is. If you're in this predicament, be sure the fact you're examining is impossible to verify, rather than too hard, expensive or inconvenient.

Just because a fact is unknowable – in business, that's most of them – doesn't prove it's true or false. This is the argument from ignorance, where ignorance means not knowing.

Absence of evidence is not evidence of absence. This means that just because you can't find any evidence or proof of something, doesn't mean it doesn't exist. So, for instance, when you're told:

"There's no evidence of [problematic conduct] in this organisation."

...you can't assume things won't come back to bite you.

Speaking of blame, causation is complicated. Be aware of the post hoc fallacy: just because one event precedes another, it isn't necessarily the cause of that later event. Few things have a single cause, even though it's easier to pin the blame on one thing or dump responsibility on one person. There are different aspects of causation:

Single cause – a single cause has a single outcome. X leads to Y. For example, a cat knocks a vase off the mantelpiece and it breaks.

Common cause – a single cause leads to several effects. That is, cause Z leads to events A and B. For example: drinking too much alcohol leads to headache, nausea, memory-loss, regret and bad tattoos.

Common effect – several causes come together to cause one result. Here C and D together cause E. Identity fraud, threat of terrorism and benefit tourism by immigrants encourage a government to try to force identity cards on its citizens.[9]

Causal chains – where one event triggers another, which in turn causes another. F leads to G leads to H. For instance: an air crash happens because bird strike damages one engine, but pilots then mistakenly shut down the wrong engine.

Causal homeostasis – where several factors work together in a virtuous (or vicious) circle to form a reinforcing mechanism. That is, J leads to K which leads to L which leads to J. For example, in the sub-prime mortgage crisis: falling house prices led to negative equity[10] which encouraged owners to abandon their home and default on mortgage payments; more foreclosures led to emergency property sales which hammered house prices.

The next time a colleague uses the cliché *virtuous circle*, correct them:

"You mean a causal homeostasis, surely?"

And whenever a colleague asserts that B was caused by A, nail down some empirical evidence that some form of causation is truly in play.

Note also that two thing that coincide are not necessarily linked (cum hoc fallacy). Correlation is not causation. When two things correlate strongly, one is dependent on the other. For instance, the market for replacement car

---

[9] All three were cited as reasons by a UK government as justification for a short-lived national identity card scheme.

[10] Where the mortgage outstanding on a house is more than the house is worth. The equity the home owners have from paying some of the purchase price with their own money has disappeared. In America, the situation is called "going underwater".

batteries is dependant on the park of aging vehicles. That is a correlation. The actual aging and usage of vehicles causes their battery to degrade, entailing a replacement. That is causation. Be sure there's an actual dependency link, not just an arithmetic coincidence.

INFORMAL FALLACIES

There are hundreds of informal fallacies that blight reasoning and argument. (For an explanation of the top hundred or so, see my other book, *Being Right: A Beginner's Guide to Logical Fallacies* on Amazon.) These fallacies make arguments weak rather than true or false.

The main offenders we encounter are faulty generalisations. This is a whole family of fallacies that reach conclusions from weak premises. Among them are cherry-picking, no true Scotsman, false analogy, misleading vividness, overwhelming exception and argument-terminating cliché.

Another broad family of fallacy is relevance. Here we find the arguments from ignorance, silence and repetition. Simple incredulity is irrelevant as an argument, as are a whole host of red herring fallacies that simply miss the point in hand. These include ad hominem attack, appeal to authority ("the chairman says..."), emotional appeals (to flattery, fear, ridicule, etc) appeals to novelty, tradition or popularity, and that perennial business favourite, the strawman fallacy.

This evergreen annoyance happens when someone misrepresents your argument as one that's easier to shoot down in flames. The way they characterise your argument usually reveals what's uppermost on their mind, but as that's not what you're saying, correct it quickly.

WHATEVER PUFFS UP YOUR LILO

Here we are. We've looked at deductive reasoning, particularly categorical syllogisms and their conditional and disjunctive cousins. These are the main expressions of deductive reasoning. Between them, they encapsulate the process of deductive reasoning. There's more to learn, if that's your bent. But for the purposes of a good education, you're done. In fact, you now know more about deduction and logic than most managers and academics.

If you're in business with aspirations of management, you have my permission to feel a little self-satisfied. Apart from a small number of specialists who understand programming logic, or have a background in mathematics or philosophy, you're now your company's go-to person for deductive reasoning. How you choose to advertise the fact is up to you.

But you'll need to be on your toes. You'll encounter formal arguments dressed up in natural language. They'll seem to be exempt from deductive rigour and deconstruction. However, wherever a deductive argument is wrongly expounded, the conclusion is invalid; if a premise is less than factually true, the conclusion is unsound.

Also, beware bare assertions of fact that are nothing of the sort. Management likes to portray itself as decisive, so managers are prone to statements that seem to display incisive thinking. Managers may present statements as categorically true, but often they're not. Be especially sensitive to claims about what will or could happen. Unless the events to come are inevitable, then they are speculative and hypothetical. Uncertain events are not deductively sound. By all means prepare a backstop just in case, but don't be persuaded that a conclusion based on a possibility is a valid or necessary step.

You'll now be alert to conditional arguments. They'll come at you thick and fast. Check the truth of *if* and *then* statements, because more often than not one or both will be wrong, which makes any conclusion unsound. Often they will reflect what an individual believes is the case, or wants it to be (wishful thinking). The fallacy of necessity will crop up more often than you can imagine. Reminder: being decisive is not the same as being right.

So that's it. You're done. Relax. Light some scented candles and slip into a warm, soothing bath, or crack open a beer and slam some death metal vinyl on the turntable – whatever puffs up your lilo.

Wear your learning lightly

Remember this?

> If you're already a respected professional or business manager, and steward of millions (perhaps tens or hundreds of millions!) of other people's piastres, not to mention the livelihood of many, many employees, and you're unable to think and reason logically, then you have no business taking the money they pay you.

Congratulations on making it this far. You've read explanations and followed examples of all the main deductive fallacies. You're now in the 0.1 per cent of people who understand the rigour of deductive reasoning.[11] Enjoy that salary – you deserve it now.

---

[11] That 0.1 per cent figure is a bare assertion. I have no idea what the true number should be, but it's not a big one. Picture yourself at a sports stadium with 50,000 spectators. Over the PA, they say there's a logical emergency, and is there anyone conversant with deductive reasoning. Will more than 50 people rush to the fore? No, I don't think so either.

I hope by now you're in a position to see the world a bit more clearly. If so, you'll know other people see a different world to you. And by now you'll know that most of the time they're wrong. You're seeing poor arguments and reasoning all around you. Well, you were warned.

Now that you know the basics of reasoning, you've passed your driving test, so to speak. You can go out on your own, deal with the changing traffic conditions, the different roads, the wild variety of drivers around you. You only truly learn to drive after you've passed your test. So it is with reasoning.

Make a note of fallacies you come across, even if you can't pin the exact one down immediately. Try to reformulate what you've heard as a syllogism – categorical, hypothetical or disjunctive. If nothing else, it'll serve as a personal party game. Over time you'll become adept at spotting invalid, weak and unpersuasive arguments, and you'll become more sure of your footing in dealing with them.

Bear in mind that you now have an intellectual advantage over most other colleagues. Be gracious. Explain and elucidate, where you can. Wear your learning lightly.

From now on, you can expect to be right a lot of the time. Enjoy it.

INDEX

abduce, 17

abduction, 12

abductive reasoning, 16

Absence of evidence, 92

affirming the antecedent, 62

affirming the consequent, 57

antecedent, 56

argument, 8

argument from ignorance, 92

bad reasons fallacy, 76

base rate fallacy, 77

bloots, chots and dips, 6

burden of proof, 91

categorical proposition, 22

categorical syllogism, 10, 20

Causal chains, 93

Causal homeostasis, 93

causation, 92

Common cause, 92

Common effect, 92

conclusion, 11, 21

conjunction fallacy, 83

consequent, 56

Correlation is not causation, 93

deduction, 12

deductive reasoning, 18

denying the antecedent, 61

denying the consequent, 59

disjunct, 71

distributed, 46

dollar-driven dreams, 91

drugs tests, 80

e**ither... or**, 74

exclusive premises, 52

exclusive-or, 71

existential fallacy, 31

existential import, 42

face-recognition software, 79

fallacy, 9

fallacy of necessity, 68

false negative, 79

false positive, 79

Figure 1 syllogism, 27

Figure 2 syllogism, 28

Figure 3 syllogism, 28

Figure 4 syllogism, 28

figures, 27

four terms – fallacy, 44

Grands Fromages, Les, 76

historically risible film *Braveheart*, 78

hypothetical syllogism, 55

if and only if, 68, 75

if**... then**, 75

illicit major, 50

illicit minor, 51

illicit substitution of identicals, 84

imply, 11

inclusive-or, 72

induction, 12

inductive reasoning, 13

infer, 11

intensional context, 85

major premise, 11, 21

major term, 25

masked man fallacy, 84

middle term, 25

minor premise, 11, 21

minor term, 25

mnemonics, 30

modal contexts, 85

modus ponens, 62

modus tollens, 59

necessary and sufficient, 67

necessary conditions, 64

necessity, fallacy of, 64

neighbour's noisy dog, 72

neither... nor, 74

non sequitur, 9

not both / not and, 75

o**nly if**, 75

particular statement, 41

piastres, 4, 96

predicate, 23

premise, 10

probability, appeal to, 76

proof by example, 81

propositional attitudes, 85

quantifier, 22

scientific theory, 17

Single cause, 92

singular premise to an
    existential conclusion, 82

slippery slope, 15

subject, 23

sufficient conditions, 66

sweet, kindly mother, 79

the worst cocktail in the
    world, 73

type **A**, 22

type **E**, 22

type **I**, 22

type **O**, 22

undistributed middle– fallacy,
    45

universal proposition, 41

you're fired, Lebowski, 81